A Story *of* Blind Spots, Insight,
and Breakthrough Leadership

THE POWER OF
FEEDBACK

Also by Susan Bixler

The Professional Image
Putnam Publishing

Professional Presence
Putnam Publishing

Take Action!
Co-author Lisa Dugan
Random House

The New Professional Image
Adams Media

5 Steps to Professional Presence
Co-author Lisa Dugan
Adams Media

The New Professional Image, 2nd Edition
Adams Media

A Story *of* Blind Spots, Insight,
and Breakthrough Leadership

THE POWER OF
FEEDBACK

SUSAN BIXLER

CEO OF BIXLER CONSULTING GROUP

with Steve Underwood

Westchester Publishing
Atlanta, Georgia
2011

Published by
Westchester Publishing
www.WestchesterPublishing.com
Atlanta, Georgia

770-953-1653

ISBN 978-0-615-45910-3

Book website: *www.thepoweroffeedback.com*
Company website: *www.bixlerconsulting.com*
Author's email address: Sbixler@bixlerconsulting.com

Disclaimer from Author and Publisher

To my son Christopher

Reviews for *THE POWER OF FEEDBACK*

"As both a business book and a novel, it's a great read loaded with significant insight. Easy-to-digest, it provides a distillation of decades-long 360 research and experience. THE POWER OF FEEDBACK is a worthy investment for any professional eager to improve his/her leadership and effectiveness. I highly recommend!"

—Jim Holthouser, Global Head of Embassy Suites and Full Service Brands Hilton Worldwide

"THE POWER OF FEEDBACK is an engaging story that draws you in with anticipation because the characters are so real and edgy…It's only later that you realize you've explored the positives about 360-feedback, as well as watched the characters overcome their blind spots and derailers. A quick read, that packs a super learning punch. I highly recommend this book for any individual or group with an honest desire to get better at what they do–feedback is key and this book unlocks the secret."

—Linda M. Kricher, Ph.D., SPHR, VP, Human Resources, McKesson Corporation

"I really liked THE POWER OF FEEDBACK! Especially for people like the character in the book named Jim, who find the thought of reading another dry, repetitive leadership development book (replete with charts, graphs, and special lingo) so daunting that they will forsake it rather than advance their leadership skills. The richness of the story and the characters help the reader fly through the book, and more importantly, retain what's been read. There is much in the book that strikes so perilously close to home it makes one squirm as the characters confront their honest feedback. There is even more in the book, however, that builds a compelling case as the characters begin to accept the value of honest feedback and grow their leadership abilities by acting on the feedback."

—Melanie M. Platt, Senior Vice President, AGL Resources

"Susan has mastered the ability to tell a story while teaching us the value of feedback and how to communicate it with honesty and humanity. It is well worth the time to read it and utilize the 360 Assessment at the end of the book for self assessment."

—Dr. Ramie Tritt, MD, Atlanta ENT, Sinus, and Allergy Associates

"I have read all of Susan's books and was looking forward to this one. It is a departure from her usual style, but it works! THE POWER OF FEEDBACK is a fresh new approach to getting at the heart of feedback and what to do with it, without being disabled by it. And for me, a business novel is much easier to read after a long day than a how-to book. She knows what she is doing because she has coached managers and executives since 1980."

—Darren Morgolias, President, Margolias Realty Group

"THE POWER OF FEEDBACK is a great way to introduce fiction into a non-fiction subject. Providing good feedback is one of the most difficult challenges of leadership. I have read this book twice and we are using the 360-Assessment in our company."

—Dirk De Vuyst, President, International Marble Industries, Inc.

"We all have blind spots and we need others to help us understand what we are overlooking. THE POWER OF FEEDBACK looks at the journey of seven characters in a fast paced company. The story provides a keen insight into why feedback is such a powerful tool to personal growth."

—Alan Lowe, President, The Lowe Group

"Knowing Susan and her work for over a decade, I highly recommend THE POWER OF FEEDBACK as a must read for all companies—both large and small. Her examples ring true and her advice and outlook on coaching is woven throughout the book."

—Greg Kenith, President and CEO, Flooring Design Group, Inc.

"A refreshing story about using strengths and overcoming weaknesses. THE POWER OF FEEDBACK has been highly motivating to both my team and me. A must read for building a team."

—Jeffrey Moore, CEO, Avery Partners

TABLE OF CONTENTS

Collier Energy is a young company in California that
manufactures and sells solar panels. As each of the seven
senior team members are introduced, their idiosyncrasies
and individual styles become apparent immediately. The
Chairman of the Board makes a surprise announcement
that the entire team will take part in a 360-Degree Report.

Larry Wesley, President, experiences the worst day of his
professional life, as his 360-Degree Report comes as a
complete shock. Revelations include:
- His supersized ego.
- His inability to convey and inspire team vision.
- His elitist attitudes, both inside and outside the workplace.

Jim Sroka, COO, learns that he needs to become more
knowledgeable about the energy business. He finds that:
- People in the company believe he lacks industry-specific
  knowledge.

- He is afraid of trying to learn more at this stage of his career.
- Yet Larry and the board consider him the strongest succession candidate for president.

- His office is a disorganized mess.
- His appearance is sloppy and at the bottom rung of business casual and doesn't convey the look and style of a senior-level executive.

Penny Boykin, CFO, struggles to properly execute. Her 360-Degree Report indicates that she:
- Does not plan in advance and many on the team are frustrated with her inefficiency.
- Barely meets deadlines on time.
- Overwhelms her team with last-minute directives.

Larry asks Paige, the leadership coaching consultant, to attend Collier's annual leadership retreat, where she'll lead a workshop based on the 360-Degree Report.

The Collier team travels to a resort in Utah for their retreat. Each leader continues to mull over his/her assessment results.

Paige meets with the leadership team and walks them through their 360-Degree Report. The group breaks down into two-person sessions for further discussion.

Mark questions his lack of Professionalism in a discussion with Abby.

Abby is skeptical of her feedback on Building Talent as she pushes back with Mark.

*"We know what we are,
but know not what we may be."*

—William Shakespeare

ACKNOWLEDGMENTS

LIKE MOST GOOD THINGS in life, it is a team that makes things happen. My "board of advisors" for this book includes many friends, colleagues, family members, and clients. My heartfelt thanks to each of you.

Steve Underwood, David Zarzour, Chris Porto, Nicolle Provost, Brandee Rees, Lisa Dugan, Margaret Brake, Shelley Hammell, Tracy Penticuff, Jody Bradham, Lisa Mackey, Marcella Woodall, Caroline Ngo, Judson McNatt, Joey Bixler Clifton, Larissa Bixler Stein, Donna Bixler, Mary Yates, Claire Bowen, Margarita Porto, Lynn Seligman, Landon Bixler, Ken Rapp, Doug Mason, Vonnie Stegner, Kap Siddell, and the amazing gang at 388 Alumni. And forever to Mama B and Papa B.

INTRODUCTION

NOTHING WILL GET your attention like a 360-Degree Report. Nothing will narrow the gap quicker between how you see yourself and how others see you than feedback. Few things in life require more courage than asking for honest feedback from those who know you best. Without it, you can't grow yourself or your businesses.

In our coaching practice, we have worked with thousands of clients using the 360-Degree Report. Those who took their feedback to heart and made changes over time, have grown into remarkable managers, executives, and highly successful leaders. Many have literally changed their lives, personally and professionally.

I wrote this book not as a "how to" but as a story. It's fictional, so I could make up the characters and the company. But they are all based on real life.

The seven people you will meet here have significant strengths and clear opportunities for improvement. Although these characters are fictitious, the blind spots, the rationalizations, and the egos are very real. You will find your coworkers, your boss, even yourself, in these pages.

You will see some of the characters stunned by their 360 feedback while others knew it before they read it. Some are angry, some in denial, some have received so much feedback in their lives that they aren't interested in it any more. But each will need to come to terms with how they are being perceived and what changes they are willing to make to be better leaders.

At Collier Energy, a cutting-edge renewable energy company, the organization is led by seven people: **Larry** the President, **Jim** the COO, **Melissa** the SVP of Engineering, **Abby** the SVP of Sales, **Doug** the SVP of Human Resources, **Mark** the CIO, **Penny** the CFO, and **Paige,** their coach. *(To learn more about each character, please visit them on LinkedIn.)* Each person on this team takes the 360-Degree Assessment, not because they want to but because the Chairman requested it. In doing so, they change their lives and those around them.

So how do you apply their experiences into your life? How can you get tangible value and an ROI for your investment and time? At the end of the book is a **Self-Administered 360-Degree Assessment**© to ask for and receive your own feedback. Based on asking 28 questions to your team, your circle of peers, colleagues, and supervisors, you will be able to better understand your impact on others and your leadership style. Your 360-Degree Assessment, completed by people who know and care about you, is the most direct way to claim your future. This is a big claim, but it works.

In our coaching work at Bixler Consulting Group we have discovered that most of our clients learn that others see more positive characteristics, strengths, and capabilities than our clients see in themselves. It's only when we identify and use our strengths, and work to overcome the derailers that get us off-track, that we build an interesting and meaningful career that sustains us for a lifetime.

But first, the story of seven people and how 360-Degree feedback changed their lives.

Chapter 1

Meet the Team

LARRY WESLEY waited in his car for the garage entrance to open, impatiently drumming his fingers on the leather steering wheel. He entered the building complex and navigated the Tesla sports car to his designated space next to the building's entrance. As he eased the car into his reserved spot, Larry smugly admired the sign suspended on the wall just above the sedan's spotless hood: "Larry Wesley." A title would have been redundant. Everyone knew who Larry was: the president of Collier Energy Corporation.

Larry entered the building's lobby and swiftly strode through the softly lit space, his footsteps echoing off the Italian marble floor. Larry always enjoyed that sound. It seemed to convey success and money. He entered the waiting elevator and pressed the button for the top floor...his floor. As the elevator began its quiet ascent, Larry appraised himself in the mirrored doors. Sporting the fruits of a trip to Italy, Larry liked what he saw. A Brioni suit, a Ferragamo tie, Gucci shoes and a Patek Philippe watch would tell people all they needed to know about Larry. He was a man of great taste and substantial means.

Collier Energy was making tremendous inroads into the nascent world of renewable energy. The fledgling company was fast becoming a major player in an industry that was poised to explode during the next decade and beyond. Growth seemed inevitable, success certain. But great expectations carry great pressure, and high bars for excellence create high levels of stress. The fault lines in his executive team were starting to show.

Larry exited the elevator and walked toward his spacious corner office. He swung open the large door, stepped inside, and turned on his computer. As he waited for the machine to stir to life, Larry considered his team. The hand selected team represented some of the finest executive talent he had encountered during his career. Yet he was sensing tension within the group. For all their talent, experience, and skills, each member had issues that were negatively impacting their peers. But, for now, the team was delivering sales results. The people issues would have to wait.

Larry skimmed his email inbox and discovered two messages from Greg Anders, Collier's Chairman of the Board. The first message, sent at 5 a.m., requested a meeting with Larry at 9:00 a.m. that morning. The second email sent at 5:30 a.m. announced an unexpected, and, for Larry, an unwelcomed meeting at 10:00 a.m. for the entire executive team. Larry leaned back in his leather chair and stared at the monitor. He considered every possible reason for such a meeting. While a few agendas seemed plausible, none seemed encouraging.

◼   ◼   ◼

JIM SROKA stepped through the lobby door entrance. An early riser, Jim enjoyed the solitude of a quiet office, a calm prelude to a busy day. Jim exited the elevator and walked through the halls, watching motion detectors switch on the lights. He made his way to the break room for the first cup of his caffeine fix.

Jim was the newcomer to the executive team, the "new kid on the block." As the COO for just three months, he was feeling overwhelmed. Although he was a quick study, he had come from another industry. The Collier team had some of the brightest, most knowledgeable minds in the industry. They were highly experienced in the energy industry and especially in solar power. Jim was having unfamiliar feelings of insecurity in his role as "number two."

Jim listened to the coffee drip into the pot. Though he was new to the office, Jim already sensed some tension among his peers. There was no single identifiable problem, he thought. No burning issues. But some team members were openly critical of each other, while others had a tendency to point fingers behind closed doors.

Jim understood that such personality conflicts in the workplace were nothing new and certainly not rare. Yet Jim himself had never engaged much in office politics, and he wasn't about to start now. His previous career as an Army Colonel had shown him that when the stakes are high, there isn't room for petty squabbling and turf wars. Maybe, Jim mused, what this team needed was some time in basic training.

Jim wasn't sure what the issues and problems were, but he was sure of one thing. Something would have to give soon.

※   ※   ※

MELISSA LOWDEN stood in her kitchen, sipping a mug of coffee, admiring the spotless space. Orderly, completely free of clutter. Not even a toaster on the counter. Sterile to some, but Melissa considered it perfect. She was the anomaly in her profession, a neat-freak engineer.

Melissa absently gazed at the flat-panel television mounted on her kitchen wall. The weather forecast was telling her something the kitchen window was confirming: it was raining—a lot. She would need to leave soon if she hoped to minimize the effects of a rainy-day traffic mess. Instinctively, she began to consider alternate routes to the office. Crowded interstates slowed by rain versus alternate roads choked by traffic lights. Which would be better? She weighed her choices. Once she got around the traffic mess, she would be faced with the office mess.

Calculations, she mused, were easy. Human dynamics? Not so easy. As the VP of Engineering, Melissa was leading a team in charge of developing some of the most innovative materials in utility production. Yet lately the products weren't so cutting-edge, as she struggled to reconcile her preference for proven models with her team's push for innovation.

Right now, her engineering team was currently under the gun to finish a prototype for a next-generation, low-cost solar panel. As the deadline loomed and scheduled signposts fell by the wayside, the other departments were growing frustrated with engineering in general and Melissa in particular. It seemed like her department was always under the spotlight.

Yet every team has issues, Melissa thought, as she rinsed her coffee mug and placed it in the dishwasher. She just represented a very high profile area. The company's insatiable appetite for new energy sources had her team chasing ideas that she just knew would never make it to the marketplace. Hadn't she personally delivered the products that had moved Collier to the head of the class in new energy? Position determines perspective. And, in this case, her peers were unable to see just how difficult her role was in comparison to their own.

Melissa grabbed her bag and keys and opened the door to the garage. It would be nice, she thought, if everyone retrained the critical spotlight on themselves.

■   ■   ■

ABBY STRYKER pressed the garage button to open the door. Directly facing her was a full-length mirror. In the garage. Abby put it there to give herself a final checkpoint anytime she left the house. As the morning light began to fill the garage, Abby admired her well-cut hair, expensive jewelry, and an elegant, yet fashion-forward outfit that would work in Milan or on Wall Street. All good. Satisfied with her appearance, Abby got into her Lexus Hybrid sedan and backed out of the garage, racing off to the office.

Abby possessed both brains and talent but she wasn't above using her looks to grease the wheels of commerce. In a man's world, she thought, a woman had to use every tool at her disposal. Charm and a killer wardrobe helped her level the playing field.

Abby turned her thoughts to the workday ahead. Today was packed with client meetings, team brainstorming, and budget updates. As SVP of Sales, Abby was responsible for pitching solar power as a viable, sustainable, and most importantly, profitable solution to the world's growing energy needs.

She was a superb saleswoman. No one at Collier was as connected to the customer as Abby. Collier's rapid growth had doubled the size of her sales team in the last 24 months. While the new team members were all competent, none was the next Abby Stryker. Abby had come to accept that her group had limitations, but she knew she was strong enough to meet her sales objectives in spite of their shortcomings. It was a challenging, but satisfying job. Usually.

But lately her workplace seemed anything but satisfying. Communication felt forced. People were frustrated with each other. Work was becoming, well, *work*. And while the company's last quarter set another record, issues were fragmenting the group.

Abby's iPhone buzzed in her leather bag. She retrieved the device and found an email from Larry requesting a meeting for later that morning. Abby slid the phone back inside her bag and considered the potential nature of a last-minute, mandatory meeting. Something was going on. Maybe changes were coming to Collier.

Whatever the change, Abby thought, maybe they could first start by adjusting some team members' attitudes. With that agenda, she would be happy to help.

■   ■   ■

DOUG LAPAR merged his car into the congested freeway traffic. With rain like this, the usual slow highway traffic became snail-like. He never understood why basic H2O could generate so much panic and caution even among good drivers. Even with his masters in psychology and 20 years in business, Doug was still surprised by clueless people. They just don't get it, he thought.

Case in point. His coworkers were a perfect example. Doug was the SVP of Human Resources so he had access to a wealth of employee information—personal and professional, official and unofficial. He was aware of every reprimand, every raise, and every evaluation. And he was still surprised that those you'd least expect could have the biggest problems. Doug felt this knowledge was great working capital. Potential chips for him to barter for more information with the people working at Collier Energy.

Doug got off at his exit and drove to his favorite coffee shop. Even though the office had its share of employee issues, he felt that his job was secure. If office gossip was any indicator, some coworkers had bigger issues than he ever would. After parking his Kia, Doug jumped from his car and raced to the café door, pausing briefly to let someone else through first. What his peers needed, he thought, was some level of self-awareness.

■   ■   ■

MARK BROCKETT stood in line and surveyed the people ahead of him. The inclement weather had brought in even more commuters than usual to his favorite café. Another coffeehouse regular entered behind Mark and dryly commented, "Great. There's nothing like rain and cold weather to bring out the masses. Now the true coffee loyalists will be late to work."

Mark chuckled politely but didn't reply. He wasn't prone to complaining, and not even rainy-day traffic and crowds could dampen his usual bright spirits.

With coffee in hand as he slid back into the driver's seat of his muddy Toyota Tundra, Mark felt his phone buzz and retrieved it from his pocket. He scrolled to his email and discovered just one message, a request from Larry for a 10:00 a.m. meeting. Otherwise, an empty inbox. And, most appealing, no complaints from people having trouble accessing their email.

As the CIO, Mark was charged with keeping Collier's technical world humming 24/7. Fortunately, his technical responsibilities ended where the people issues began. Computers were much easier to deal with than people. His role allowed him to sidestep some of the thornier interpersonal issues, and he was happy that his team enjoyed a world that was somewhat insulated from workplace politics.

Still, lately he had noticed some friction among the executive leaders. Nothing like open hostility, but there was definitely an undercurrent of tension and frustration between them. The simmering attitudes were even starting to creep into his fortified domain. Mark had always been able to use his sharp sense of humor to diffuse workplace tension. But, recently people seemed to laugh less at his jokes.

Mark slipped the phone back in his pocket. He was grateful that all that office drama fell under Doug's jurisdiction. But, if Mark were responsible for Collier's people issues, he would bring some simple, practical advice to the table. One word—*chill*—especially for the uptight male and female divas occupying the corner offices.

■　　　■　　　■

PENNY BOYKIN picked up her green tea from the service counter and headed for the door. She stood under the store's awning waiting. The moment there was a pause in the downpour, she made a dash to her car and quickly jumped inside. Penny carefully sipped her tea in the car and considered the day ahead. Her schedule as CFO was jam-packed with meetings and more meetings. The young company was currently flush with funding, as investors were clamoring to be a part of the next big thing, whatever that thing was. Investing was always a gamble, but it seemed that, in today's unpredictable energy climate, renewable solar power was a relatively safe financial bet for the long-term.

Yet, though Collier enjoyed robust financial support, her boss and everyone around her demanded more and more detailed reports. It was like an MRI, she mused, with multiple slices and views of exactly the same thing. But in reality, how many pictures were really needed? And lately the workload was growing faster than her ability to manage it. Some people clearly needed to dial down their expectations. Every day seemed to bring another fire drill. Penny didn't mind the frenetic pace. In fact, she prided herself on how well her team could function while "under the gun."

As Penny pulled into the parking deck, she was sure of one thing: her colleagues needed to refocus their attention in their own departments and leave her alone.

■   ■   ■

GREG ANDERS, Collier's Chairman of the Board, stood at the head of the conference table and surveyed the room. The executives were seated and making small talk with their fellow team members. Seated near Greg was a woman whom no one had met. Greg could feel the unspoken question buzzing throughout the room: was she replacing someone? He chuckled to himself. She wasn't taking anyone's job, he thought, but she still may not be everyone's favorite person in the coming weeks. Greg cleared his throat, and the room quieted.

"Good morning, everyone," Greg said. "Thank you for being here. I know this meeting was scheduled quickly and the emails and phone messages are piling up, so I'll be brief.

"This is Paige Darnell," he said as he gestured to her. "She is part of a consulting firm, BCI, that specializes in corporate leadership development, specifically executive coaching.

"First, let me tell you what this does not mean," he said, slowly looking around the table, studying each face. "It doesn't mean that anyone's job is in jeopardy. Or that the company is in trouble. Or that we're making sweeping changes."

Everyone seemed to discreetly exhale.

"Having said this," he continued, "I believe that our executive team could immensely benefit from some outside perspective. Because no matter how well we do our jobs and how well we work together, there is always room for improvement.

"Let me turn it over to Ms. Darnell so she can explain just what that means for Collier." Greg took a seat and motioned for Paige to address the group.

Paige stood and said, "Thank you, Greg. Good morning, everyone. And, please, call me Paige," she said. "I very much look forward to working with you. As Greg mentioned, I know you're all busy, so I'll be brief.

"Collier Energy has become a leader in renewable power, specifically affordable solar panels, in a very short time," she began. "What you've accomplished in three years is impressive and well-known in the industry. And, as you continue to grow and achieve greater success, it's important to continually evaluate what got you to this point and what can take you to the next level. It will require different skill sets and a greater self-awareness of the enormous talent here.

"Our consulting group is dedicated to helping companies achieve that next level of success. We do this by developing a company's most vital resource, its leaders. You and your team are the key to Collier's continued growth and achievement. This team is more vital to Collier's success than any product you sell.

"We do our coaching work in two primary ways," she said. "First, we provide assessments that allow you to discover your strengths and weaknesses and to gauge how you think about and approach situations and people.

"Second, we guide you through a customized assessment called the 360-Degree Report. Just as the name suggests, this personal assessment is completed by you as well as those around you."

Faces around the table conveyed concern, resistance, or curiosity. Some conveyed all three.

"Here's a simple overview," she said. "You select twelve people, from peers, to superiors, to direct reports. We then provide a customized and confidential, online questionnaire with questions for each of the raters to answer. The completed survey is then submitted to a secure, third-party website. You will be evaluated in seven key areas: Leadership, Business Knowledge, Innovation, Building Talent, Trustworthiness, Professionalism, and Execution."

Her gaze was now met with folded arms.

She pressed on. "After the questionnaires are completed, you will be provided with a confidential, detailed report with both numerical and written feedback for each of you. We call the process a "360" because it offers a complete view all around you. Again, these reports are confidential, and you will have the only printed copy.

"I know all of this may sound unnerving," Paige said. "But let me tell you about the benefits. I've headed the firm for 20 years, and I can honestly say that our 360-Degree Report can change lives and companies for the better. Quite often companies and teams fail to address the real problems that affect their business because there's no good forum for doing so. The 360-Degree Report creates an appropriate, safe environment for issues to be discussed. And, once those concerns are on the table, you benefit by the open conversations that can come only from honest feedback and transparency. You also get a great read on your strengths and talents."

Paige read a variety of facial responses: fear, skepticism, doubt, hope. These were all natural responses, all anticipated, and all of which marked the beginning of the process.

"Does anyone have any questions?" she asked.

Larry spoke up. "I do. When does this begin?"

She smiled. "Next Monday."

Chapter 2

Leadership

—noun *to create and communicate a compelling vision of the future*

LARRY WESLEY sat at his impressive mahogany desk and surveyed his office. In one corner a gleaming conference table offered privacy and convenience. In another, a leather sofa and loveseat framed an antique coffee table. Original, carefully collected art was displayed on the walls.

Behind him floor-to-ceiling windows offered a majestic view of the Pacific Ocean. Directly facing him was The Wall, where a galaxy of industry and community awards orbited the centerpiece statements, a Bachelor's in finance, a Master's in mechanical engineering, and an Executive MBA from Harvard.

It was an office that commanded respect, conveyed accomplishment, and projected success. It was a space where Larry always felt a sense of control. But an unexpected reality had scaled his executive fortress.

Larry Wesley was experiencing the worst day of his professional life.

■   ■   ■

COLLIER ENERGY was a vanguard in the growing movement to renewable energy. After the oil spill in the Gulf, awareness and utilization of solar energy was growing. Located in California, Collier developed and sold affordable solar power generation. Collier was heeding the call to find new ways to feed the world's insatiable need for safe, affordable energy.

This call was nothing new. The renewable movement began in the 1960s, though action quickly dissolved into rhetoric. But, with record highs in energy production costs and a growing instability among overseas providers, power companies were finally seeing green.

As the company's president, Larry Wesley was responsible for steering Collier's foray into this brave new world. Larry's mandate was simple: find ways to make solar power practical, affordable, and profitable.

Until 45 minutes ago, he thought he was doing a good job.

■   ■   ■

LARRY glanced at the packet on his desk. It appeared like a seemingly harmless report, just like the dozens he read each month. But this report was different. Its contents were entirely about him and his leadership.

Larry tilted back in his leather chair and considered the ceiling. Only four weeks ago, Greg had directed his departments' leadership teams to take part in the 360-Degree Assessment. Now the feedback was processed, the reports received, and the results ready for review.

Except parts of his review read more like fiction, Larry thought. Keeping up the metaphor, one chapter had been particularly devastating.

Larry wondered why this report was even necessary. Sure, there was always some friction among his team members. Staff meetings could occasionally be a blood sport. But this just encouraged a healthy sense of competition. This was big business with big stakes. Pressure was a natural part of the job. And, even if everyone didn't always mesh well personally, they got the job done and delivered results. Apparently success was not enough.

Larry had first reviewed the questions with a smirk. *Does the leader navigate the political waters in a way that creates a win-win? Does the leader have a presence in our industry?* Uh, *yeah,* he thought. That's why I'm the president. Larry believed his success spoke louder than any report. Not everyone agreed.

▓ ▓ ▓

PAIGE DARNELL stepped into a small interior lobby and approached the desk of Natalie Long, Mr. Wesley's assistant.

"Hi, Natalie," Paige said. "Is Mr. Wesley in?"

"Yes, but he said he isn't taking calls or visitors right now."

That sounds about right, Paige thought. "I understand, but I believe he's expecting me. Would you mind checking with him?"

Natalie nodded and picked up the receiver.

"Mr. Wesley, I know you're not receiving visitors, but Ms. Darnell is here to see you." Pause. "Yes, I'll send her in." She hung up the phone and smiled but cautioned, "Be gentle."

Paige returned her smile. After working with hundreds of companies, this exchange felt familiar.

▓ ▓ ▓

PAIGE opened the heavy office door and stepped inside. Larry did not stand to greet her but remained seated, facing the window.

She closed the door and looked around. Everything looked in its place, an office filled with rich appointments. The only thing missing was his self-confidence.

"Larry, thanks for taking the time to meet with me," Paige said. "I left the 360 Report for you this morning, and just wanted to check how you're doing with the feedback."

He grunted. "Assuming you've read through my report, you might assume I'm a bit shocked and disappointed."

She smiled slightly. "These reports are sometimes surprising, with a lot to absorb at once. I know. I've gone through this myself. Twice."

"Surprising?" he muttered. "Try shocking. Like stepping blind folded in the ring with a bunch of pit bulls."

"I understand," she said. In fact, she knew, the first step in this process was defined as surprise, and sometimes shock.

Larry swiveled to face her. "My entire team, even those I consider friends, had negative comments about me. *Personal* negative comments. Did you read those?" he asked.

"I did," she replied. She clicked off some comments in her mind: gracious to peers, dismissive to inferiors. Outwardly friendly, inwardly held grudges. Extremely knowledgeable, but unwilling to slow down and share that knowledge with others. Executed well, but autocratic and sometime brutal in getting what he wanted.

"How will this bring about any positive change?" he challenged, tapping the report binder.

"Change doesn't happen without confrontation," Paige replied. "I don't mean destructive confrontation, but honest and open conversations about issues. Without honesty, problems just get brushed aside, especially when a group is as outwardly successful as yours."

Larry grunted. "So why fix something that isn't broken? Sure, not everyone gets along. And certainly no one is perfect. But is this supposed change worth getting everyone worked up? Is it worth," again tapping the report, "criticizing the leadership here at Collier?"

"There were many positive comments on your leadership, Larry," Paige said. "It's easy to dismiss them and instead obsess on the development areas. But those critical observations don't negate the positives.

"Here's a suggestion," she continued. "Before we meet again, highlight in yellow every area where you got kudos. And then, use a blue marker for the development areas. I've got some highlighters right here," she said, handing him the pens. "You'll be amazed at how much yellow you'll have all over this report."

Larry rolled his eyes and took the pens.

"Larry, I believe in feedback. My whole business is based on it. And I believe the changes that will result from the 360 are worth the initial pain and frustration. I hope to prove that to you. Or more importantly, I hope you'll see the proof firsthand."

"Proof is right," he said. "But, until then, consider me a skeptic."

"Of course, I understand," said Paige with sincerity.

※　　　※　　　※

PAIGE walked out of Larry's office and closed the door. She had seen just about every imaginable reaction to the 360. Few executives or managers ever accepted feedback without pushing back, rationalizing, brushing it off, or feeling hurt.

Paige pressed the elevator button. Even with years of experience in executive coaching, she paid a lot of attention every time she worked with a client as to how the report needed to be presented. One method was to review the feedback simultaneously with the individual. Or as in Larry's case, she let him privately read the results first. Either way, the feedback report was an essential part in guiding a team toward positive changes, but the leader had to be onboard and somewhat comfortable first.

Clients resist feedback for a number of reasons. But fear was at the root of the resistance. Larry's prickly attitude and abrasive response were partly due to a bruised ego and hurt feelings. But underneath, he was probably afraid that he might be too flawed a leader for a vital position.

The doors opened and Paige stepped inside the empty elevator. She pressed the Mezzanine button and leaned back against the wall. Larry had received a large number of positive comments on his abilities. But, like most clients, Larry focused on the negative. And he was afraid of hearing remarks that were less-than-flattering, especially from those he cared about most. For now, Paige would focus on underscoring the positives.

But Larry had more surprises in store today. His most honest feedback would ultimately come from his wife.

▦   ▦   ▦

LARRY pulled his car into his driveway. The fading light filtered through the stately sycamores, casting cooling shadows over the manicured lawn. It was normally a welcoming sight when he returned home. But then today was not very normal.

As he slid his car into the garage, Larry couldn't believe how much had changed in 24 hours. Yesterday he had returned home after a 12-hour day at work and enjoyed a quiet evening. Today, while the calm setting was the same, Larry viewed it through a very different perspective.

Larry grabbed his laptop bag, shut the car door, and walked to the house entrance. Though the bag was light this evening, the report inside made the satchel feel like it was carrying lead. As he stepped through the entrance, Larry realized he needed feedback from his most honest and trusted source. He made his way to find her.

▦   ▦   ▦

TINA WESLEY sat at a shaded table by the pool on the rear patio of their sprawling home. She sipped her glass of wine and took in the remaining light reflecting off the water, enjoying the breeze moving through the terrace. It was, she thought, a perfect end to the day.

The sliding glass door opened, and Larry walked onto the patio. She immediately sensed his mood. Looming dark clouds on an otherwise sunny afternoon.

"Hi" she said. Larry didn't respond and slid into a chair. He glowered at his lush yard, usually a comforting view, but today a reminder that perspective does indeed determine attitude. What he saw today as he looked at his lawn was a ridiculous, over-manicured, money pit.

"Larry?" she prompted. "What's going on?"

Larry sighed and finally responded, "We received the results from our 360 Report today."

She silently answered her own question. *But of course.* The results didn't match his expectations. No surprise there. Her husband had a blind spot for self-awareness and his impact on others. Still, she had to ask, "And?"

Larry turned to her and replied, "Well, let's see." He held up a hand and began ticking off fingers. "My team thinks that I don't share my knowledge, that I micromanage everyone, that I hold grudges, that I have a super-sized ego, that I fail to share my vision with them, and that they don't have stock options that are commensurate in our industry.

"Oh." He threw up his hands and said, "And I'm rude to the janitor."

■   ■   ■

LARRY and Tina sat at the kitchen table, each nursing a glass of wine. Tina glanced through Larry's report while he stared at his glass. The food Tina had prepared sat untouched. Neither seemed to have an appetite.

Tina looked up and said, "Okay. This is not all bad."

Larry continued staring at his glass and said, "Okay, so here's the thing. Let's say that even 10% of the negative feedback is accurate. Let's say that my team thinks I'm some kind of egomaniac who roams the office, squashing every idea in my path. Let's say I am the bad guy in this report. What am I supposed to do with that?"

"First," Tina replied, "Not everything in your report was negative."

"Sure," he said. "I received a few gold stars. I know any and everything about our business. I'm ethical and I—let me try to quote this—'Larry never tries to gain personal enrichment at the price of his integrity.'

"I'm good to work with one-on-one," he continued, "But only if I'm with my peers in the workplace or with clients. I have a wide range of interests, but I'm also a snob. And, finally, I'm charming and gracious, but only with people at my social level." He added in an exasperated tone, "There seems to be a caveat lurking behind every accolade."

Tina nodded but didn't respond.

"So," Larry asked. "Am I an elitist jerk?"

"Well, tell me this," she said. "Do you agree that you can be charming?"

Larry considered his glass and said, "Sure. I agree with that assessment."

"And do you agree that you're incredibly knowledgeable?"

"Absolutely," he stated.

"And do you agree that your personal integrity is solid?"

"Yes, of course," Larry said, frustrated. "But Tina, what are you saying? That the positives cancel the negatives?"

"No," Tina replied. "My point is that if the positives are true, is it possible that some of the negatives could be true, too?"

■   ■   ■

TINA sat on a recliner in the living room, feet tucked underneath her, reading the rest of the report. Larry was sprawled on the floor, a cushion under his head, staring at the massive chandelier overhead.

After some time had passed, Larry stirred. "So, can you imagine getting feedback like this? I can't see how these reports will help office morale and production. How can they?

"More than that," he continued, "I consider some of these people my friends. Instead they just seemed to be waiting for the right moment to throw me under the bus. "

Tina set the report in her lap and looked at him. "Larry, I know you're shocked and mad, but you're exaggerating. I think your team actually showed they cared by being fair and honest with you. They actually took a big risk."

He propped himself up on one arm and looked at her. "But loyal team members wouldn't make such harsh comments about their leader."

"Maybe, maybe not," she replied. "But think of *how* they made these comments. They shared them in a way that made them vulnerable. They've never tried to take you down out of spite. They were asked to be honest in these confidential reports, and they did that. Maybe it's a compliment to you that they are willing to risk your anger, and even potential payback, to share what they believe will help you and the company."

Larry sighed and rolled onto his back.

"Okay, then," Tina said, "Let's see if we can find some truth to these 'personal attacks.'" She picked up the report and read aloud, "Larry is very social, and is charming and gracious to peers and colleagues. Yet he often takes a condescending approach to people who are not on his social or professional level." She laid down the report. "Do you find any truth to that?"

"Do *you* find any truth to that?"

"Just for a moment," Tina said, "Consider what that means. Do you know the names of the security guards at the building? Do you know the faces of anyone in custodial? Do you greet the guy who takes care of our pool, who has been coming here once a week for almost ten years?"

She continued quietly, "Or think about when we go to a restaurant. You barely acknowledge the server, but you're very friendly with the owner. So yes, you can come off as a bit elitist."

Tina continued, "But Larry, you are so gracious when you want to be. You can entertain executives and clients and charm anyone in your path. If you want to."

"So I'm supposed to change my ways?" Larry asked. "I'm supposed to become a man of the people and hang with the hourly workers? To just magically change overnight?"

Tina considered her response and then said, "I don't think that's what this is about."

■   ■   ■

LARRY sat at the kitchen table, the report resting in front of him. It was well past midnight, and Tina had gone to bed. He closed his eyes and listened to the insistent tick of the wall clock, quietly reverberating in the still room. Larry opened his eyes and opened the binder, determined to make sense of the report.

The biggest shock, he thought, was not that his coworkers and boss were critical of his leadership, although that certainly qualified as surprising. What troubled him was the gulf between his self-perception and the perspective of those around him.

One example: Larry had graded himself a 4 (on a scale of 1 to 5) in the category of "Sensitive to satisfaction and morale within the team." His average peer score? A 1.98. *Less than a 2.* Everything in him argued that this must be a mistake. But there it was in black and white, staring at him like an indictment. He made a mental note to ask Paige if direct reports were the toughest rater group.

Next, "Communicates an inspiring vision of the future." His score, a 4. Everyone else? An average of 2.62. Is it even possible, he wondered, that a seasoned leader could fail to share the company's vision? What had he been conveying all these years? *A future marked by fear and filled with few opportunities for his team and the company?* This perception seemed completely at odds with his record of success. Yet there it was. His 12 raters collectively believed that he failed to cast and share an inspired vision.

This assessment was, without a doubt, one of the most unsettling in his career. Was he really in need of that much improvement? Sure, there were some positives. "Holds each team member accountable for results," scored a 4.8. "Sets clear expectations," a 5, the highest possible score. But these traits fell under generic Leadership 101. The real sting came from the low scores and the comments on issues that felt distinctly personal in nature.

And, while some comments were positive, others were less-than-flattering. "Driven by power and recognition. Micromanager. Holds grudges." This report wasn't suggesting evolution, but great personal flaws. And would the change be worth it? Even great leaders have great flaws. History proved that.

Though Larry was angry, he was rational enough to know that arguing was futile. Regardless of his self-perception, 12 people did not agree with his personal assessment of leadership. Six team members, 1 CEO, 3 customers, and 2 executive assistants. And when you're outvoted by 12 to 1, there must be some truth to the majority's perspective.

But is it possible, he wondered, that I simply don't communicate who I really am? Maybe people don't know the real me, he thought. Even if this was true, the problem remained. People believed he was deficient in critical areas of leadership behaviors. So there remained only two options: Either he was simply misunderstood or he had some very prominent blind spots to address.

Larry stood and turned off the kitchen light. He made his way to the bedroom, although he knew sleep would be elusive. He remembered a question from a leadership session he had attended several years ago. "What's keeping you up at night?" Tonight, he knew the troubling answer.

Chapter 3

Knowledge

—noun *expertise in the key technical*
aspects of the job

JIM SROKA was uneasy. After a military career and then more than 15 years of mid- and senior-level leadership positions in two different start-up companies, Jim was entering the next phase of his career. Gone was the constant turmoil of unstable teams. Gone were most of the 12-hour days, the daily crises that pulled him away from friends and family and cost him two marriages. It was a time to savor all he had accomplished and enjoy a relatively smooth ride to a comfortable retirement.

As Collier's COO, Jim was a large part of the company's daily operations. Jim viewed his role as maintaining processes and structure. Others in the company, he learned today, took a different view.

They felt he was maintaining the status quo, partly because he didn't know much about the energy industry, especially solar energy. Others believed he fell short in supporting new ideas for Collier and also in making recommendations for new products. Both were areas that fell outside Jim's interest, knowledge, and expertise.

Sitting now in his office, Jim glanced at the report on his desk. Part of Jim's job was to prepare for the unexpected, a skill he had acquired in the military and regularly put into use. Part of being prepared, he knew, was being self-aware. Jim had always prided himself on being completely honest about his pluses and minuses. So overall the results of his 360 report weren't surprising.

Except for one small, and in his opinion, relatively unimportant section.

■   ■   ■

PAIGE stepped off the elevator and walked toward Jim's office. *Day Two.* Paige greeted various employees as she navigated the hallways. By all appearances it was business-as-usual, and people's outward attitudes seemed to reflect that.

Yet she also sensed an undercurrent of unease and tension. The fallout from the 360 reports would not be readily noticeable, she knew. People were still absorbing the results, considering the feedback, and, most importantly, discussing their report with those they most trusted. People generally resisted change, especially personal change.

Paige approached the desk of Jim's assistant.

"Hi Stacy," she said. "I have a 9 o'clock meeting with Mr. Sroka."

"Just a sec," Stacy said, calling Jim. She listened, nodded, and then said, "Go on in."

Paige opened the door to Jim's office. She knew it would be an interesting conversation.

■   ■   ■

PAIGE stepped into Jim's office and closed the door. Jim, on the phone, nodded at her and held up his index finger, asking for a moment.

Paige nodded back and surveyed the room. Jim's office stood in sharp contrast to Larry's. His furniture was several steps down from luxurious. The older and uncoordinated furnishings suggested that Jim preferred function over form. Sports memorabilia bobble heads, trophies, and fan photos covered the walls and lined the shelves.

But just like Larry—or any executive, she thought—the wall facing Jim reminded visitors that this was in fact a person of accomplishment. Framed awards, citations and certifications hovered together like comforting sentinels. Unlike Larry, however, Jim did not attend schools usually associated with executive leadership. He began his career in the Army, where he parlayed his service into a GI Bill-funded degree at a respectable state university.

What Jim lacked in Ivy League pedigree he made up through discipline, devotion to getting the job done, and commitment to his team and customers. Jim's 360 report flashed through Paige's mind. He was considered dependable, considerate, and he met deadlines. He took responsibility and didn't pass blame on to others. All in all, he was well liked by his peers. And most of all, he probably saw no reason to change.

Jim's development, she knew, would be both simple and very challenging.

※   ※   ※

JIM hung up the phone and stood to greet Paige.

"Sorry about that," he said, shaking her hand. "Have a seat," he continued, indicating a slightly cracked leather chair facing his desk. "Can Stacy get you anything? Coffee? Water?"

"No, thanks," Paige replied, sitting down. "I'm all set. Good to see you."

"Good to see you, too." Without preamble he began, "If you don't mind, I'd like to jump right into this. And I've got some questions for you."

Paige nodded and said, "Absolutely."

"I know you have done hundreds of these," Jim continued. "So I imagine that my results aren't unique. But this is the first time I've ever gotten this kind of feedback, so I'm still trying to figure out what to do with it. "

"Okay," she said. "So, what are your thoughts? What were you already aware of and what is surprising to you?"

"It's pretty much what I expected," he said, placing the report on his desk. "Preparation. The Boy Scouts taught me that, the Army reinforced it, and my professional life has made it a mantra. I like to think I'm self-aware enough to be honest about my faults and strengths."

"That's a rare gift," Paige remarked. "You had positive comments almost across the board."

"Well, I appreciate that everyone feels I'm doing a good job. It's very satisfying. But, and this may sound trite, I get the most satisfaction from getting things done and meeting deadlines. That's why I'm here, right? To keep things moving and operating on schedule."

"Yes," she agreed. "And your report reflects your commitment to excellence." Paige paused and said, "There is, however, one area of opportunity that could trip you up and diminish your effectiveness."

Jim leaned back in his chair and said, "Right. I don't have a tremendous depth of knowledge about our industry."

Paige nodded. "Do you agree with that assessment?"

Jim shrugged. "Sure. It's true that I'm new to this industry. But, really, nearly everyone in this company is new to renewable energy.

"And," he continued, "manufacturing is manufacturing. We're certainly not trying to reinvent the wheel on that front. So, really, in my area of the company, industry-specific knowledge doesn't seem that important. We have all kinds of geniuses running around the office who are doing the actual development."

Paige considered her response. "I understand. You definitely have some people here who are on the cutting edge of these technologies. But your teammates believe that you could benefit by learning more about the field."

"That's true to an extent," he said with a dismissive wave of his hand. "But again, I think I'm progressing just fine. No one here understands every facet of the business. We're learning as we go along. And sure, I'm lacking some of the knowledge my teammates have, but it'll come in time."

Jim's office phone buzzed and he picked up the receiver. He listened and said, "Be right there."

Jim placed the receiver down and said to Paige, "Sorry to cut this short, but Larry needs to see me right away." He added with a smile, "Just a small crisis this time." Jim glanced at his desk calendar, another nod to an old-school mentality in a high-tech world. "Could we reconvene in about 30 minutes?"

Paige smiled and nodded. "Sure, Jim." She stood and walked toward the door. Paige paused as she opened the door and said, "But do me a favor. Just think about the positives of increasing your industry knowledge. How that could benefit you professionally. And how it could benefit your team."

Jim nodded and said, "Will do," while thinking, *I've got enough to worry about.*

░   ░   ░

PAIGE walked to a temporary office that Collier had provided, allowing her to work without having to leave the building. She took a seat behind her desk. As was usually the case, Paige was beginning to feel a little more like a partner and a team member and less like an external consultant. She was learning more about their culture, their roles, and the tremendous opportunity they had as pioneers in their industry.

Paige sipped from a water bottle and reflected on her first meeting with Jim. Just as she had expected, Jim wasn't interested in making changes. More so, he didn't think that gaining knowledge was even necessary. Jim functioned well in his role and had done a satisfactory job by every measurable standard.

Industry knowledge, however, was subjective and not measurable by any real standard. It made perfect sense that he would consider this issue irrelevant, Paige thought. Jim existed in a professional world and mindset of Six Sigma guidelines, ISO certifications, and LEED. Some things that could not be easily defined, like depth of knowledge, was nebulous and, therefore not important to Jim. He knew enough, he got results, and that's all that mattered. Yet Jim's peers believed that his lack of knowledge was detrimental to both himself and the team.

The question, Paige mused, was this: Was Jim truly indifferent to this issue? Or was his insecurity hiding a fear of change or even a fear of having to learn so much at this stage in his career?

◼   ◼   ◼

JIM knocked on Larry's open office door.

"Jimbo," Larry boomed. "Come on in. We've got a little problem here."

"Okay," Jim replied, feeling tension slowly grip his body. "What's up?"

Larry handed Jim a binder. "Here's the report your team did for my preliminary association meeting tomorrow. It seems there might be a few holes in it. I'm not sure they checked their analysis and got the facts right. Did you read this?"

Jim opened the report and realized he didn't completely understand the product in question. "I did, but…," Jim trailed off. He asked, "When are you leaving tomorrow?"

"10 a.m."

"I'll get it right," Jim assured him. "Count on it. You'll have it before you leave tomorrow."

"Okay. 10 a.m. tomorrow." Larry appraised Jim a moment. "One more thing." He paused and said, "I'm curious about your take on this 360 thing." He added casually, "Interesting reading, huh? Did you learn anything new?"

Jim cleared his throat. "I did, yes." Jim considered a moment and directly replied to the underlying question. "My teammates indicated that I could stand to learn more about our business. Not from a process perspective, but knowing exactly how our solar products work."

Jim looked at the binder Larry had given him and said, "I thought this was accurate information, but I honestly couldn't be entirely sure. I focus on the bigger picture and lean on my team for the specifics. That approach seemed to be working."

"Okay," Larry said, framing his face with his thumb and forefinger. "If you don't mind, would you share some of your feedback from the 360? In a general way."

Jim leaned back. "Sure. I did well overall, I think. I mean, I got positive feedback in most areas. I get the job done, meet deadlines, respect and support my team." He smiled. "I basically do my job, which is a relief to hear."

"Right," Larry said. "You absolutely do, no question about that." He thought a moment then said, "What about this suggested area of improvement? What are you going to do about it? "

"Well," Jim paused, considering his reply. "There seems to be a consensus that it would benefit the team if I learned more about our specific energy sector and product line."

"But," he rushed on, "I *am* learning. This whole industry is still in the early stages, and few people are an authority on anything. It's going to change and go in unexpected directions anyway. We don't even know which energy source will be the dominant choice, you know? And since Collier has product experts and researchers who will always know more than me, how much do I really need to know about solar?"

"Right. But," Larry paused and said, "well, do you want my feedback?"

Oh no. "Yes, of course."

Just then Larry's phone buzzed. He looked at the display and said, "Hey, this is Greg. Let me grab this."

▩   ▩   ▩

JIM stood and wandered over to a large bay window that looked out at the ocean. He tuned out Larry's conversation and thought about this impromptu meeting that had quickly gone from casual to serious. *Note to self, next time have the head of engineering review any reports that go to Larry.*

Since the comments in his 360 report almost universally mentioned his lack of industry knowledge, Jim knew that Larry agreed with, and had contributed to, that assessment. Yes, he could stand to learn more. Jim knew there were industry classes, sessions, even entire conferences, dedicated to sustainable energy. It wasn't that off-the-job learning was difficult. It just seemed unnecessary.

But if he were honest with himself, Jim was insecure about the idea of learning about an entire industry at this stage of his career. His professional makeup was firmly planted in an old-line work ethic, just work hard, don't complain, and get the job done. This attitude was a proven formula for success that had worked for him all his life. What got him here should continue to work for the rest of his career.

But Jim also understood that a new world was emerging. A world where information and technology was as critical as work ethic. A fast-paced place where you could quickly become a relic if you didn't have access to the most up-to-date knowledge about your industry. Working hard and delivering results would always be the foundation for anyone's success. But, in this brave new world, was he working hard on the right stuff?

※　　※　　※

LARRY hung up the phone and motioned Jim back to his desk. "Sorry about that."

"No problem," Jim said, settling back into his chair.

"So, your 360." Larry thought a moment.

"When it comes to knowledge, I tend to agree with what you indicated in your report," Larry said. "Now don't get me wrong. You're incredible at your job. You bring a wealth of experience to our team. You're a rock for me.

"But," Larry continued, "it's critical that our COO be well versed on sustainable energy. It's critical for a few reasons.

"One, employees look to you, as a leader, to be on the forefront of what's happening in the industry and at our company.

"Second," he continued, "your pursuit of growth and knowledge will inspire those employees to push themselves to grow.

"Third, even though we're still in the designing, developing, and approval stages of operations, the time is approaching when manufacturing will fully go online. Right now is the most opportune window to learn as much as you can before your time is consumed with keeping everything running.

"And," Larry paused. "there's one more critical reason."

Jim cleared his throat. "What's that?"

Larry replied, "I believe that with the right knowledge and understanding of this business, you could take your career to the next logical step."

Jim shifted in his chair. "Where do you see me going?" he asked.

"Well, one option is this office," Larry said, theatrically gesturing with his arms. He joked, "How about this view?" Then in a more serious tone, "Come on, Jimbo, I know you've considered that possibility."

"I mean, maybe," Jim said. "But really, Larry, I enjoy working under your leadership. I don't have any desire for that to change."

"Jim," Larry leaned forward, propping his elbows on his desk, making a teepee with his fingers. "Greg won't be the Chairman forever. He's eyeing retirement in a few years. It stands to reason that I would be in line for succession to his role." *If this 360 thing doesn't become my professional obituary.*

Jim slowly nodded. "Right."

"And if that happens," Larry continued, "I can absolutely see you being groomed for *my* role."

Larry's phone buzzed again. He looked at the display and said, "Greg again. Look, let's try and meet later this week. We can review the updated investor's report together. Maybe lunch on Friday. Good?"

Jim stood to leave and said, "Absolutely. Lunch would be great. Thanks, Larry."

Jim opened the door and experienced another wave of tension. *Do I even want to take the next step?*

■   ■   ■

JIM navigated the hallways and made his way to the break room. He needed a moment away from his office to think.

He walked into the empty room and headed straight for the coffee pot. As he poured his coffee into a mug, he reflected on his conversation with Larry. He wasn't entirely surprised by Larry's succession comments. Deep down in thoughts unspoken, he had considered the possibility of becoming Collier's president if Larry became the CEO.

Now that Larry had verbalized the idea, albeit casually, the prospect took on an entirely new dimension. As the president Jim would need to understand almost every facet of Collier's business, including the industry and the market place. This would require learning a tremendous amount about the industry, and fast.

But was that even possible? Jim wondered. Manufacturing was one thing. Becoming an industry expert was quite another. Manufacturing existed in a very clear, defined space. It was a linear, finite world where Jim felt comfortable. Learning about, and keeping up with, a rapidly changing industry seemed daunting at this stage of his career.

Jim started back toward his office.

▓   ▓   ▓

JIM turned the corner to find Paige outside his office.

"Hi," Jim said. "Sorry about cutting our meeting short."

"No problem at all," Paige said. "Let's keep going."

Jim and Paige stepped into his office and he shut the door. They both took their seats.

"Okay then," he said, leaning back in his chair. "Believe it or not," he started, "since we last met, oh, 20 minutes ago", he smiled, "I've actually had some time to consider the gap in my knowledge of this business."

"Wow, you work fast," she said. "That's great. What are your thoughts?"

"Well," he said, "If I were being completely honest here, I would have to admit that I'm a bit intimidated by learning a new industry at this stage of my career. Old dog, new tricks, you know?"

She nodded. "I do. It can seem daunting."

"Right," Jim said. "Daunting is a good word for it. And, I have to admit, I'm still not entirely certain that I need to go all-out to gain knowledge about this industry. There are a lot of reasons. But, simply put, I'm not entirely sold on the idea that it's necessary for my current role."

Paige raised an eyebrow. "Current?"

"Yeah, see, that's the rub," he sighed. "I'm realizing that if I want to take my career to the next level. I would need to better understand how wind, water, and natural gas complement solar. One of my team members recently sent me an annual report on a large supplier of natural gas in the Southeast that indicated the U.S. alone has 100 years of natural gas available at current U.S. consumption. So for solar to be relevant, I need to understand what can fill the void when the sun isn't shining."

"You're right," Paige agreed. "More knowledge takes you to the next level, and your growth will encourage everyone on the team to grow, too. It's not what we say to our team, but what they observe in our actions and behaviors."

"Right," Jim grudgingly agreed.

"Deciding to make a change is easy. It's *sustaining* change and growth in our lives that's the challenge," Paige said.

Jim's phone buzzed and Stacy's voice came over the speaker. "Mr. Sroka, your 11 o'clock conference call is about to start."

Jim offered an apologetic smile. "Sorry. This morning has turned out crazier than I expected."

Paige stood and said, "Don't worry. I'm here at your convenience. I'll work with Stacy to set another meeting."

Jim watched Paige leave. *But how much work is this going to take? Do I have the mental capacity to learn all I need to know in time?*

Chapter 4

Innovation

—noun *flexible and open to new ideas and different approaches*

MELISSA LOWDEN sat at her desk and noted the time on her computer screen. *6:51 a.m. And 31 seconds.*

Melissa's professional world hinged on precision. The engineering team was in the process of conducting beta tests on products that were the future of Collier. Big pressure, she thought, with very small margins for error.

By habit, Melissa unconsciously continued her countdown. *6:54 a.m.* She glanced around her office, a testament to an organized mind. The room was sparsely furnished save for one extravagance: Hundreds of manuals and reports lined the walls, all made orderly by large, mahogany bookcases. And she had read almost every one. Melissa was the company authority on all things solar and sustainable including wind and natural gas energy. She understood the engineering positives and negatives of going solar, hydro, and everything in between.

6:56 a.m. Melissa recognized that she had a key point of view in every product approval process. Her team could give the green light on a new solar device or prevent a next-generation panel from moving into production. The process from design to production was tedious for some. But Melissa lived and breathed the details. Or, what some might less charitably consider, the minutiae.

6:58 a.m. Yet there was a flipside to her precise nature. These very traits could also cause her to appear controlling, inflexible, and resistant to risk. Plus, her demand for perfection was causing collateral damage.

6:59 a.m. And 28 seconds.

▦   ▦   ▦

PAIGE walked to Melissa's open office door and knocked on the frame.

"Hi, Paige," Melissa said. "Come in."

"Hi, Melissa," Paige said as she stepped into the office. "How's your morning so far?"

"Good," Melissa replied crisply. "Gearing up for some production meetings later today. Got some big deadlines looming."

Paige nodded. "I know this is a crazy time for you and your team."

"That it is," Melissa agreed. "Please, have a seat."

Paige sat facing Melissa and looked around the room. "Everyone should be this organized," Paige said. "This is impressive!"

"Yeah. I'm a bit of a perfectionist," Melissa said. Skipping the formalities, Melissa abruptly addressed their agenda with a focus and directness that caught Paige slightly off guard, "And I'm not the only one who thinks so. I'm assuming you've seen my 360 report."

Paige replied, "I have. But just me. When it comes to our 360 clients, we only provide one report directly to you."

Melissa nodded.

"So," Paige said, "what are your thoughts?"

Melissa pulled her report from her desk filing cabinet. She flipped through the binder and said, "Okay. Here. The negative comments were primarily in the Innovation section."

"Try not to think of the comments as just negative," Paige suggested. "Think of the comments as insights into changes you can make in your role. Changes that can enhance your job. Even maximize your efficiency."

"I'm all about that," Melissa said. "But these comments and low scores in innovation seem anything but positive."

"I know it can seem that way at first," Paige said. "But think about when you did the assessment for others. I bet your motivation was to help them, not hurt them. To help them see themselves in a different perspective."

Melissa nodded. "Yes. I didn't have any personal agendas."

"Right. And I bet that everyone who made these comments had a similar motivation," Paige said. "To help you succeed at what you do here."

Melissa didn't respond to that statement, but said, "Let's take a look."

※　　※　　※

TERRY LAWSON timidly knocked on Melissa's doorframe.

Melissa looked up and frowned. "Hey, Terry, I'm in a meeting."

As a senior designer, Terry was all too familiar with Melissa's response to change, be it in a meeting or otherwise. "I know, Melissa, and I'm sorry for interrupting. But I have a very quick question that needs an immediate answer."

Melissa sighed and said to Paige, "Could you give us a moment?"

Paige nodded. "Of course." She stepped outside the office.

"What is it?" Melissa asked.

"Our solar panel project," Terry began, already dreading the answer. "It's supposed to go into production in a little less than 60 days."

"I think I recall that," Melissa replied dryly.

"Well, my contact at WAV, our solar cell provider, just called and said they just now approved—literally yesterday—a new cell that improves on what we are now using." Terry rushed on. "We could improve our energy efficiency model by 10%. A huge jump. It leaps over any current industry standard."

"For the next product version?"

Terry braced himself. "I was thinking we could try it on this model."

Melissa leaned forward. "This one?"

"It's possible," Terry said. "More than possible, actually. WAV can overnight the components and we could be testing tomorrow afternoon."

Melissa was shaking her head.

"I know it seems like a tight window," Terry said. "But we have enough time for testing. We're already ahead of schedule. We can use that margin for further testing." He quickly added, "And changing the cell doesn't require that we change any other components. It's all still compatible. We're just changing one aspect."

"Just one?" Melissa snapped a little sharper than she intended. "I would consider the cell the most important part."

Terry nodded. "It is. But WAV has done extensive testing on the cells. They're ready for production. And they could give us a big jump on the competition. No one else would have that level of energy efficiency in the marketplace except Collier."

Melissa sighed. "Terry, I appreciate your enthusiasm. And your commitment. But there is no way I'm switching anything on that product at this stage of development. It's entirely too risky."

"But we have so much time—"

"Terry," Melissa cut him short. "We're going to proceed with the current model as planned. We're already passing the industry standard by 1%. We'll consider new technologies during our next project. Okay?"

Terry couldn't hide his disappointment, but nodded. "Okay." He turned and left her office.

"Paige!" Melissa called out.

Paige walked through the door. "Problem solved?" she asked, taking her seat.

"No. Problem prevented."

▩   ▩   ▩

MELISSA'S desk phone buzzed. She glanced at the display and said, "Excuse me, Paige. This is Larry."

She picked up the phone and said, "Hi, Larry." She nodded to herself and said, "No. No problem." *But it will probably become a problem.* "I'll be right over."

Melissa set down the receiver and said to Paige, "Is *that* a problem?"

"Not at all," Paige said as she stood. "Can we meet up again later today?"

▩   ▩   ▩

MELISSA LOWDEN knocked on Larry's office door. She heard Larry's muffled "Come in," and opened and stepped through the door.

"Hi, Larry," she said, closing the door behind her.

"Melissa," he said, "have a seat."

She sat down across from him and waited for him to begin.

Larry tapped his phone. "I just got a call from Tad Baylor, the president at WAV, with great news. They just approved a new solar cell that is a huge leap from their current component."

This sounds familiar. Melissa nodded. "I heard that this morning."

"Right. WAV wants to strengthen their partnership with us. So they're giving Collier exclusive access to the cell before anyone else—even the media—learns about it. After that window, it's every company for itself."

"That is great news," Melissa agreed.

"Yes." Larry picked up a schedule. "But it gets better. I then realized that we are ahead of schedule on our current solar project. And judging by this schedule, it seems possible that we could even use that cell in this project. We could be the industry leader in solar products before our competitors knew what hit them." He smacked the desk for emphasis.

Melissa cleared her throat. "I considered that, Larry. But unfortunately I think it's too late to make changes at this point."

"Oh?" Larry laid down the schedule and frowned. "Why? Tad, who should be informed since he heads the agency, notified me that the new cell is compatible with everything else in the project. What are the challenges involved?"

"Time, primarily."

Larry looked at the schedule. "I admit that I don't know every facet of engineering. But it seems to me it's entirely possible. In fact, we have almost the same amount of time available for component testing as we did originally."

"Maybe so," Melissa replied. "But that's assuming there won't be any resulting issues."

"Okay. Simple fix," Larry said. "If it doesn't work, we revert back to the original model."

Melissa wouldn't budge. "But then I'm potentially wasting precious time and resources for something that could fail."

Larry appraised Melissa and leaned forward. "Why are you resisting this? It's such a small risk for something that could produce big dividends. Huge. It could boost our image. Make us the product leader. Bring on new customers. Just imagine. We make a late-breaking announcement just as the panels are ready to go online. The entire industry would notice."

Melissa didn't reply.

Larry saw that Melissa wasn't convinced. "Look Melissa, I appreciate your perspective, but I'm going to have Tad send over those cells immediately. We can't afford to squander this chance. I know you don't entirely agree, but I need you to do this."

Melissa didn't reply but nodded slightly.

Larry would normally have a stronger reaction to an attitude that bordered on insubordination. But there was no denying Melissa's intelligence and extraordinary level of industry knowledge. And Larry believed that brilliance and eccentricity were closely related. So Melissa generally received a free pass in human relations.

"Okay, then" Larry said. "Let's schedule daily meetings this week so I can stay informed of your progress." He paused and added, "This could be amazing, Melissa."

Melissa nodded weakly and left the office.

◼   ◼   ◼

PAIGE glanced at the small clock on her computer screen. 10:52. With someone like Melissa, she mused, it was best to err on the side of being early.

Paige considered their brief meeting earlier that morning. Paige understood that engineers were naturally very logical and detail-oriented. These traits made them good at their jobs. But the flipside of those traits was a tendency toward perfection. The temptation to be controlling. Getting mired in analysis paralysis. Detail-orientated to the point of obsession.

The attention to detail could even affect their management style, as they may feel compelled to micromanage every aspect of a project and team. Melissa's 360 report communicated that her team definitely felt micromanaged and she hated suck-ups and resisted any compliments from her staff. So it was hard to build a relationship.

Yet Melissa's team considered her to be highly competent. Everyone around her, in fact, from her team to her peers to Larry, highly regarded Melissa's talent in her role. She had a prominent hand in developing some of Collier's next generation power components.

Paige stood and walked out of the room toward Melissa's office. The key, Paige understood, was helping Melissa loosen her grip on her projects and on her team. To find peace in letting things be less than perfect. And to help her realize that these changes could improve her performance and the team's morale.

■　　■　　■

AT 11 a.m., on the dot, Paige again knocked on the doorframe to Melissa's office.

Paige realized that Melissa seemed less enthusiastic than earlier that morning. "How are you?"

"Well, I was fine when I got up this morning. Or at least better than I am now." She looked down at the report. "Anyway. Let's look at my report."

"Okay," Paige said. "Let's talk about it. Do you know what stands out to me on your report?"

Melissa shook her head, fearing the worst.

"Your incredible range and depth of knowledge," Paige said.

Melissa looked up, startled.

"This falls under the 360's Knowledge section," Paige said. "Here, your average scores are off the chart. Your peers recognize that you're one of the most knowledgeable people at Collier. You are *the* authority in the office on sustainable energy and how solar fits in. People depend on you to understand very complex technologies and issues. In short, you're a vital part of this team."

Melissa slowly nodded her head. "I do love to learn everything I can about new energy. It's kind of a passion of mine." She added sheepishly, "Sounds lame, right?"

"Not at all," Paige replied. "Collier needs people that are passionate about emerging technologies. They couldn't even stay in business without people like you."

Melissa again nodded her head. "Okay."

"Something else that stands out in your report," Paige continued. "You scored very high under Trustworthiness. This involves all kinds of traits and behaviors. For example, you are considered sincere and straightforward. This is such a compliment to you."

"I try to be, anyway," Melissa said.

"You are also considered very responsible," Paige continued. "One comment specifically said that you always accept responsibility for your group, even if someone else on the team makes a mistake. So you can tell they hold you in very high regard."

"Well, I appreciate that," Melissa said. "They're an incredible group of people. But it's hard to hear the good in the report when the bad seems so loud."

"I understand," Paige said. "But remember, what seems bad is actually people just trying to help you see areas where you can grow. Think about what we've just talked about. People consider you very knowledgeable about this industry, and invaluable to Collier's initiatives and products.

"People also consider you very trustworthy," Paige continued. "Your team in particular knows they can trust you to represent and lead them. So when you take these viewpoints into account, realize that people think highly of you. And because they do, it stands to reason they only want good things for you. To see you do well and grow, right? And maybe be willing to accept an affirmation on good work, when warranted."

"That makes sense," Melissa grudgingly agreed.

"Now, with that in mind," Paige said, "let's take a look at some areas in which there's room for growth."

■   ■   ■

MELISSA and Paige sat next to each other on chairs facing Melissa's desk. Now a bit more comfortable with her assessment, Melissa held open the report between them.

"Your areas of opportunity revolve around Innovation," Paige began. "This section involves a few different traits, like risk-taking, stress behaviors, and how people handle pressure."

Melissa nodded and said, "My meeting with Larry was actually about taking risks. Not directly, I mean. The meeting was about something else. But we did talk about risk.

"I don't understand the issue with risk," Melissa said. "I work in a very controlled environment. There's no room for error. The products have to be as precise as humanly possible. People expect perfection from my department. And then," she complained, "they turn around and ask me to take risks that threaten that perfection. It doesn't make any sense."

"I understand that," Paige replied. "Maybe Larry and your team want you to take more *calculated* risks."

"But most risks just seem to outweigh the benefits," Melissa said. "Even the word implies the chance for failure. And I don't have room or time for failure."

"Behind every great success," Paige said, "you'll probably find a hundred failures. Nothing good happens without risk. In our jobs or in our relationships. Everything requires some degree of risk." Paige then suggested, "Maybe you could work with Larry to find a mutually acceptable margin of risk that works for both of you."

Melissa frowned and said, "I don't know how wide those margins could be for me." She looked at her report and switched topics. "On another note, my team seems to think I micromanage them. These comments really sting, because I try so hard to be a good leader."

"But remember," Paige reminded her, "your team recognizes that you're a great individual of high integrity. Try to view these comments with that in mind. So in that context, why do you think they feel you micromanage them?"

Melissa thought a moment. "I guess because I'm very hands-on in every part of the development process. Not much happens in my group without my direct knowledge. But, ultimately, *I'm* responsible for everything that leaves our department and goes into production. So I need to be as involved as possible."

"Considering your level of responsibility, it's natural to feel a sense of ownership over these projects," Paige said. "It's important to remember, however, that people on your team will need to feel an increasing sense of project ownership to grow in their roles. And they need to know that you trust them to do the job well."

"I do trust them," Melissa said defensively. "It's just I need to be involved at every level."

"How about this," Paige said. "Just as you would meet with Larry about risks, why don't you meet with your team to find ways in which you could help them feel more ownership? You might find a middle ground that feels right for everyone involved."

Melissa looked uncertain. "I don't know. I'm not very good at gray."

▩   ▩   ▩

JIM SROKA was on a phone call when he saw an instant message from his assistant Stacy jump onto the screen. *Melissa is here to see you. She wants to know if you're available.*

Jim considered the request. While he and Melissa met throughout the week, they usually stopped to talk only when the other's office door was open. It was unusual for her to interrupt him when his door was closed, the universal sign for "I'm Busy."

Jim spoke into the phone, "Hey, would you mind if I called you back in a few minutes? Great, thanks." He hung up the receiver and walked to the door then opened it. Leaning out he said, "Hey, Melissa, come on in."

Melissa walked in and sat in front of the desk. Jim sank into his own chair and took a quick reading on Melissa. She seemed upset.

"I'm sorry to interrupt you," Melissa said. "Thanks for seeing me."

"Of course, Mel," Jim replied. "What's going on?"

Melissa sighed. "I'm just having a bad morning. A bad week, actually. First the 360 report and then a terrible meeting today with Larry."

Jim didn't respond about the meeting but said, "Those reports are certainly eye-opening."

"I don't mind telling you about my report," she said. "It probably won't even be surprising to you. It basically says—or I guess my peers say—that I'm a perfectionist. That I'm inflexible. That I avoid risk. And, worst of all, that I micromanage my team to death."

That sounds right, Jim thought, but said instead, "Certainly they said some positive things, too. You're very respected in the office."

"They did," Melissa replied. "But the negatives just feel so shocking." She continued, "And then Larry called me about a new solar cell at WAV."

Jim nodded. "I heard that. Exciting news."

Melissa grimaced. "It is. But *now* is not the right time to implement any changes in our panel. We're too close to production to make *any* radical changes."

"So we're not moving forward on that?" Jim asked.

Melissa rolled her eyes. "No. We are. I am, in protest. I can't really argue with Larry."

"That's true," Jim agreed, then quickly changed subjects. "So, what's your next step in the 360 plan?"

Melissa answered with another question. "Where do I even begin?"

Chapter 5

Building Talent

—verb and noun   *identifying strengths, weaknesses,
and developing people for the next level*

ABBY STRYKER made her way to her office at Collier Energy, cutting a formidable swath through the corridors. Her entrance was striking, energetic, and high on style. From her chic hair, to her well-cut trouser suit and her Manolo Blahnik heels, Abby looked successful and confident.

She greeted employees, offered waves to people across the cubicle farm, and conferred smiles on the masses. But Abby's bulletproof persona hid a growing level of anxiety. And annoyance.

Abby said good morning to her assistant, Brooke, and entered her office. She tossed her bag onto the leather sofa and settled into her desk chair. As she waited for the computer to boot-up, Abby looked around her office. She took in the carefully collected antiques, original art, and tasteful accoutrements. Abby was a master of image and was able to navigate the fine line between fine quality and obvious opulence.

She was scheduled to meet with Paige Darnell this morning to discuss her 360 report. Abby was less than thrilled about this conversation. She was a cornerstone of the company, the rainmaker, and, next to Larry, the most visible face of Collier Energy.

And yet, in spite of those realities, she was considered deficient in team-building skills. Abby struggled to understand just what that meant. Abby felt she shared praise (when it was due), recognized effort (when it was deserved), and listened well (when it was important). Besides, her track record spoke for itself. Did Collier prefer perfection or results?

After mulling her report, Abby decided to commiserate with her biggest fan. She jumped up and left the office.

■   ■   ■

ABBY strode into Larry's office; appointments were unnecessary for her. Larry, holding the phone to his ear, smiled and said into the receiver, "Hey, let me call you back." He set down the phone and said, "Well, good morning, Abigail."

"King Lawrence," Abby replied, "how goes it?"

"The subjects are growing restless," he said, sliding his 360 report off the desk and holding it up.

Abby rolled her eyes.

"Right," Larry said, tossing aside his report. He stood and indicated the sofa. Abby sat while he took the loveseat. "So, what's up?" he asked.

"Well, certainly not my team's morale," she joked. Then in a serious tone, "I'm concerned about this 360 report. I had some good scores, but I came up short in Building Talent. Seriously? Really? I can't even make sense of that."

"Abby," Larry began, "did you and your team exceed projections last quarter?"

"Yes," she replied.

"And the quarter before that?"

"Yes," she said, emphatically.

"And you're on target to beat them again this quarter?"

"Absolutely," she said.

"There you go," Larry said, dismissively waving his hand. "Look, let's put this 360 report in perspective. You are one of the shining stars at Collier. You're a highly visible face and representative of the company. You press the right flesh, mingle with the right people, and connect with the right clients. As far as I'm concerned, you're exceeding expectations."

Abby smiled. "I'm glad you think so, Larry."

"Everyone thinks so," he said firmly.

"But, still," she said, "let's imagine, for argument's sake, that this 360 report has some measure of validity. I mean, it's one thing for one person to make that kind of statement. It's quite another for the majority of my raters, especially my direct reports, to agree."

"Okay, so, maybe you address that issue going forward," Larry said, drumming his fingers on the arm of the loveseat. "But, again, you've got to keep this thing in perspective. Yes, grooming talent is important. Yet you have a fantastic team already. And your numbers speak volumes about the kind of work you're doing. The kind of work your team is doing."

Abby nodded. "Right."

"This is a crucial time for Collier," Larry said. "It's vital that we sell our products and build our client base. You are absolutely essential to what we're doing and where we're going. So don't stress out about this report. Keep doing what you're doing. We're a young company. There'll be plenty of time to build talent."

"Okay," Abby replied. She stood to leave and said, "I've got a meeting with Paige this afternoon." Abby paused at the door and smiled. "So I may be back before the day is over."

■　　■　　■

PAIGE approached Brooke's cubicle, which was located just outside of Abby's office.

"Good morning, Brooke," Paige said. "How's your day so far?"

"Good, thanks for—"

"Paige!" Abby exclaimed, rounding the corner. "So good to see you," she said, offering her hand. "Great outfit! You're supposed to help me, not upstage me." She shook Paige's hand and said, "Come on in. Would you like anything?"

"I'm good, thanks for asking," Paige said, smiling at Brooke. She followed Abby into her office. "I thought I'd stop by this morning and say hello."

"Excellent," Abby said. "Let's adjourn to the sofa, shall we? Less stuffy."

Paige sat down and said, "Abby, you always look terrific. Those shoes are fabulous."

"I picked them up in New York," Abby replied, settling into her end of the sofa. "I travel there about once a month on business, so I make a point to fit in some shopping, too."

"Very nice," Paige enthused. "New York has the best shopping in the world."

"It's part of my job to enhance the Collier image both inside and outside the company." She laughed. "It may even be in my contract." Abby paused then said, "So, I've briefly skimmed through my 360 report."

Paige nodded. "And? Your thoughts? Reaction?"

"Confused. Conflicted. Annoyed," Abby laughed. "I scored very well in Professionalism, Execution, and Knowledge. Which all seem like prerequisites for the job, right?"

"Yes," Paige agreed. "You received universal praise in those areas."

"Right," Abby said. "Then I read the Building Talent section and it's like those compliments don't exist. I can't believe people actually view me that way."

"I understand," Paige said. "It's important to realize, though, that these comments are not meant to hurt you. So while the critical comments can be tough to take, know that your team basically wants more development time with you. "

"Maybe. But I'm still not sold." Abby laughed.

"Believe me," Paige said, "I've done many of these assessments. And I can confidently say that the 360 is also beneficial for identifying strengths, not just weaknesses."

Abby smiled. "Well, I always go with the expert opinion. And since you're our coaching guru, I guess I'll take your word for it."

Abby glanced at her wall clock and said, "I'm glad you stopped by. Let's spend about an hour reviewing this at our scheduled 3 o'clock."

"Of course," Paige said. "Today is all about you."

"And I just love that," Abby said.

※　　※　　※

ABBY walked into the restaurant and spotted her best friend, Paula Nichols, already at a booth. Abby walked over to the booth and gave Paula a quick hug.

"Paula, so glad you could do lunch," Abby said, sliding into her side of the booth. "You are my 'last-minute client appointment' and excuse to skip out early on a meeting."

Paula laughed. "I'm so glad I could help. Boring meeting?"

"Actually, the opposite of boring," Abby said, glancing at the menu. "I'll tell you all about it."

The server arrived and they placed their orders.

Paula sipped her water and said, "So, not boring. But a need to escape from...?"

"Remember that report?" Abby asked. "The 360 assessment that we had to take at the office?"

"Yeah. It's like a report card but you don't have to get it signed."

Abby laughed. "Exactly. In this case, I got mostly As, a couple Bs, and one big fat D."

"In what?" Paula asked.

"Building Talent," Abby said with a dramatic flourish. "Apparently I spend too much time selling products and making money and not enough time stroking the egos of my team."

"You've got to be kidding me," Paula said.

"Oh, no," Abby said. "It reads like a diva's novel in that particular section."

"Sounds like fiction to me," Paula remarked. "We're talking opinions here, not necessarily facts."

"This is true. But in the business world, perception is everything. And the perception at Collier is that I don't invest in and build my team. That it's all about me and I don't share credit with anyone on my team. That I'm not grooming the next Abby Stryker. "

Paula laughed. "I don't think the world can handle more Abbys. But, really, you can't be taking this report seriously. What did Larry say?"

"Larry seemed to shrug it off," Abby replied. "He said the numbers are what's important. And, in that area, I unequivocally deliver."

"So there you go," Paula said. "The boss, and your biggest advocate, thinks the 360 report isn't important in the scheme of things."

"True." Abby paused and said, "And, let's be honest, there's probably some sexism here. My team is mostly comprised of men. So, what, because I don't pal around with the group and talk sports I'm not investing in their lives?"

"Right," Paula said. "Maybe you could start playing fantasy football with them."

Abby laughed. "Oh yeah. My team-building scores would go through the roof." Abby considered a moment. "Thanks for talking with me about this. I was starting to take that report too seriously."

"Please," Paula scoffed. "You deliver big results. You make the big deals. People love you. Larry knows how invaluable you are to Collier. This report does nothing to take away from that. Don't let some random opinions, which could even be motivated by jealousy, bring you down."

"Thanks, Paula," Abby smiled. "What would I do without you?"

"You'd start believing your bad press. Can't let that happen to my best bud."

⬛   ⬛   ⬛

PAIGE sat at her desk composing an email. While she was looking at the screen, her mind was elsewhere. She thought about her abbreviated meeting with Abby.

On the surface, Abby seemed open to coaching and pursuing ways to grow. But Paige sensed an undercurrent of skepticism to the idea of changing any of her behavior. Her peers probably saw nothing wrong with Abby's performance. Some aspects of her job were easily measured, such as sales goals. Abby apparently had no problems in that department. But it was the other areas, such as building, encouraging, and grooming her team, which offered no simple barometers for success.

While she was considering this, an email from Abby popped up in her inbox. *Hi Paige, see you at 3. –AD.* Paige replied that she would be there and hit Send.

Paige realized that, in spite of Abby's confidence, and even arrogance, regarding the 360, the report had almost certainly found a chink in her armor. Now Paige just needed to help Abby see how the report could help her.

◼   ◼   ◼

"Hi, Brooke," Paige said. "I have a 3 o'clock meeting with Abby."

Brooke nodded and said, "Abby said to just go in."

"Thanks." Paige walked to Abby's office and peeked inside. Abby noticed Paige and waved her in.

"Paige, come in, come in," Abby said. "I'm just finishing up an email. Give me a sec and I'll meet you back at the sofa."

Paige took a seat and glanced around the room and took in every furnishing, every seemingly casual touch that was in place by design. Yes, Abby was a master of image and presentation. But was there anything beneath the polish, the sales pitch, the charm? Paige believed there was. Getting Abby to acknowledge—let alone discuss—her concerns was the challenge.

◼   ◼   ◼

"OKAY," Abby stood and walked to the sofa, holding her 360 report. She took a seat, placed the report next to her and said, "Sorry for the delay. Sales is no respecter of persons. And it certainly is no respecter of my schedule."

"I can imagine," Paige said.

Abby sat back and said, "It is a wild time right now. So much is happening. I have a big contract waiting in the wings that could really increase our presence in the marketplace. It's a crucial time for Collier, certainly for my sales."

Paige nodded.

"So, when you consider Collier's growing pains and the pressure on the sales department to deliver, this report is not my top priority," Abby said, tapping the binder. "I don't mean to cause offense, but I want to be straightforward with you."

"I appreciate that," Paige said.

"My top priority," Abby continued, "is sales. To establish Collier as a force in our marketplace. To score big contracts, to make the right deals, even to attract the right type of funding. This is the all-consuming, bottom-line mission that drives me." Then, as an afterthought, she added, "And leading my team."

"Of course," Paige said. "But—"

"Also, if I can be completely honest," Abby pressed on, "I don't think this report would look the same if I were a man. I know that's a standard-issue, broad, all-inclusive statement, but it's true. Certainly you can understand that."

Paige considered her reply. "To a degree, yes. But the reality is you *are* a woman in a business environment. And, yes, gender may be an influence. However, the bottom line is that, regardless of gender being a pro or a con, it's there and we have to deal with it."

"I agree," Abby said. "I'm just saying, for the record, between us, there may be some attitude in this report that's a result of that reality."

"Remember, though," Paige said, "you received very high scores in other areas. Building talent is a very specific section. For you to receive uniformly similar marks in that one area suggests that either A) There's a general consensus on the issue, or B) There's a conspiracy against you." Paige smiled. "Now which sounds more plausible?"

Abby didn't reply.

"I could believe it was motivated by malice if you received one or two random comments," Paige continued. "But 10 people, including your team, generally agreed that this was an area in which you could grow. Would that make it at least worth exploring?"

Abby slowly nodded. "Okay," she said, her tough façade giving way to a slight smile. "Are you sure you're not in sales, Paige?"

Paige laughed. "Far from it."

"Well," Abby said, "I'm not entirely sold, but I'm willing to hear your pitch."

■   ■   ■

ABBY sat facing Paige on the sofa, the report now open in her hands.

"I don't quite get the team-building issue," Abby started. "In sales, you've generally got it or you don't. I mean, you can certainly refine and improve those skills. But they're sales people because they are good at what they do already. What exactly am I supposed to do to make them better?"

"Making sales is certainly an art." Paige agreed. "It definitely helps to have the right style and disposition to be an effective sales-person. Your role in developing your team is twofold. First, you invest in them. Not babysit them or tell them what to do. But share your knowledge, your skills, and your insights with them. And ask questions and get their opinion on different accounts and maybe how they handle objections and push-back on solar power."

"That's tougher than it sounds," Abby said. "You have to under-stand, sales is a very competitive environment. Even though we're on the same team, we're still in a sense competing with each other."

Paige nodded. "Right. But it's important to remember, your ulti-mate service is to the company. And part of that is making the sales team as effective as possible. Or, think of it another way. Your team's performance is also a reflection on you. So it would serve you well to help them maximize their potential growth and performance."

Abby didn't directly reply to that but said, "And my second role in development?"

"To develop your team members for advancement." She added with a smile, "To even recognize and groom your replacement."

Abby forced a sharp laugh. "To find someone to replace me? Did I mention this was a competitive job?"

"You did," Paige said. "But consider this. If you invested in your team, would it enhance your relationships with them? Would it cultivate a stronger bond? By doing that would you strengthen relationships? And if you had stronger relationships with them, why would they want you replaced?"

Abby cracked a smile. "Wait, doesn't everyone think like I do? I mean, I just assumed the smart people did."

Paige smiled. "Think of it another way. You'll eventually be ready for the next phase in your career. You'll eventually want to move from sales into broader, and larger, responsibilities, right?"

"That's the plan," Abby agreed.

"Would you say Larry invests in your growth?"

"Absolutely," Abby replied. "He's been a big advocate of mine."

"So," Paige continued, "does Larry's interest in helping you grow inspire you to plot for his job? Or does it inspire feelings of camaraderie and loyalty?"

Abby seemed to mull this over.

"Or think of it another way," Paige said. "What if Larry operated out of fear instead of consideration? What if he had the attitude of protecting his turf? If he viewed his people as threats instead of assets? How would that make you feel?"

"That does make sense." Abby paused and said, "I'll confess, Paige. Before this meeting, I was ready to write off this report."

Paige nodded.

"Now," Abby said, and paused again. "Now, I have some thinking to do."

Chapter 6

Trustworthiness

*—noun   demonstrating integrity by keeping personal
and company information confidential*

DOUG LAPAR slowly inched his car through the drive-thru. This
fast food chain wasn't his normal first choice. He usually preferred
being around people in a more sophisticated coffee house environment. But he wasn't feeling very social this morning.

Doug had received his 360 report this week. The results were a
revelation, to say the least. He had received some great comments
and compliments in numerous areas. Yet one section was dynamite
and seemed to blow up everything else.

Trustworthiness. Doug considered this category the most personal
of the bunch. Knowledge. Building Talent. Execution. These were

all areas that could be addressed and developed by someone. They weren't inherent traits, but learned skills.

Trustworthiness was different. It encompassed traits that were part of a person. Even defined someone. To say that Doug was untrustworthy was saying he had a somewhat flawed character. And how do you fix that?

Doug approached the service window and held out his debit card. He received the card back with his latte. Regardless of the report, Doug was determined to keep his game face on. He would figure this out, and no one was going to see that the report had affected him.

As Doug drove away and entered the street, he wondered how anything good could possibly come from this assessment.

▧   ▧   ▧

DOUG walked through the office, greeting everyone around him. He unlocked his office door, flipped on the lights, and turned on his computer. Doug walked to the window and took in the parking lot below. The view wasn't as commanding as Larry's, or even Abby's. But his corner office would someday come. *Unless this 360 report hurts my chances.*

"Dougster!"

Doug couldn't help but crack a smile. "Abby," he said, turning to his guest. "What brings you to this side of the building?"

"Just wanted to see how the other half lives." She laughed as she walked through the door. "Plus, I needed the exercise. The coffee house accidentally used whole milk instead of skim in my latte this morning. Who even drinks whole milk anymore?"

"Calves?" Doug asked dryly. He took a seat behind the desk and asked, "What's going on?"

Abby took a seat opposite him and said, "Just this little thing called the 360 report. You've heard of it?"

Doug smiled weakly. "I think so."

"Yes. Well, Mr. HR and resident career counselor, I did well in most every category," she said. "Except for one: Building Talent. Which is frustrating."

"Well, but you can address that—"

"It's especially tough to take because our team is firing on all cylinders," Abby said. "If you were an innocent bystander and observed our department, if you placed us in a bubble and made a study of our performance, you would think we invented world class business development."

"You mean you didn't?"

Abby laughed. "Don't tell anyone." She thought a moment and said, "But really, this report has made me think. I mean, I still think our team does an incredible job. And, honestly, I'm a big part of that. I've brought in some major contracts in the last few months. It's hard to believe that one small report could make that seem unimportant in comparison."

Doug nodded. "I get that. But it seems easy enough to fix. Well, not easy. Maybe just simple. Clear. Defined. Something you can address by taking planned, purposeful steps."

"Dougster," Abby said with a laugh, "I'm too busy selling the future of energy."

"There is that, yes," Doug said, leaning forward on his elbows, lacing his fingers. "Did you talk to Larry about this?"

"Oh yes," she replied. "Yesterday, in fact."

"And?"

"He seems to think it's a non-issue," Abby said. "Said my numbers speak for themselves."

"And what about Paige?"

"Paige," Abby said, considering her reply. "She's actually made me think about all of this a little differently. I would be more dismissive of the process and the results, if it wasn't for her."

"How so?" Doug asked.

"She's done this for more than a few companies and for a lot of years," Abby said. "And she believes that the 360 report, when done with honesty and consideration, will enhance the individual and the team. It's at least worth hearing her out."

Doug didn't reply.

"Not to say that any of this is easy," Abby said. "I'm still not entirely sold on the fact that I'm deficient in this area." She laughed and said, "Or any area, for that matter. Have you seen my numbers?"

"I may have heard something about them."

"Right." Abby paused and said, "Maybe my team just needs more coddling than I believe necessary. And it's frustrating that I have to slow down and waste time helping people that should be able pull it together on their own. I hate going through their proposals and having to make edits."

"Yeah, but some of them aren't in great shape. Paul's wife just filed for divorce, and it's going to be nasty," Doug said, referring to Paul Hutchins, a Sr. Director of Sales.

"You're kidding," Abby said, leaning forward, eyes wide. "When?"

"About a week ago," Doug said. "He's been pretty shocked and out of it ever since. Looks like his wife has already moved in with her boss. Yeah, it's going to be a mess."

"Great," Abby said. "The last thing I need right now is someone whose life is a reality show." Abby stood and said, "Life happens, right? And Paul isn't the only one who has ever gone through a divorce. Hopefully he'll be able to leave the ex-wife issues at home."

"True, but—"

"Okay, Douglas my friend, I need to get back to work. Thanks for the news update." She walked toward the door and, as an after-thought, turned to Doug and asked, "How about you? Doing good?" She began to turn before he replied.

"I'm great. Fine. Yep. Thanks."

Doug leaned back in his chair and stared out the window.

DOUG entered the break room to get another cup of coffee before his 11 a.m. meeting with Paige. As he walked through the door, he noticed Melissa sitting alone at a table, drinking a cup of coffee, devouring a scientific journal.

"Good morning, Mel," Doug said. "Some light reading there?"

Melissa looked up and replied, "Sort of. Just learning about the next generation of photovoltaic cells for use in commercial solar energy production."

"I read all about that last night," Doug joked.

Melissa smiled.

Doug poured his coffee and pulled up a chair opposite Melissa. "How's it going?" he asked.

Melissa placed a bookmark between the pages and closed the journal. "Fine," she replied. "It's been an interesting week."

Doug sipped his coffee and asked, "How so?"

"This 360 thing, mainly," Melissa said then paused. "Basically, my team feels that I stifle creativity. That I squash new ideas. Ouch."

Doug nodded. "I heard about that."

Melissa looked startled. "You did?"

"Well," Doug said, "Just from a couple of people. Privately. I mean, it's not office gossip or anything."

"You actually heard that?" Melissa asked, mortified.

"Yeah," Doug replied, "But look, this wasn't from the higher ups. I mean, it's not like I hang out with Larry on the golf course or anything. Some of your team mates may have mentioned it."

Melissa absently nodded, her face betraying her unease. "I met with Paige this morning to discuss my report. We talked about my low scores in Innovation. Specifically about my apparent inability to accept new ideas." She thought a moment and asked, "Did Paige happen to talk to you about my report?"

"No, absolutely not," Doug replied. "Anyway, I wouldn't worry too much about being singled out. The 360 has been a big deal for everyone." He glanced at the open door and said quietly, "Even the bulletproof Abby."

Melissa's eyes widened. "Really. In what area?"

Doug pulled back. "I can't say," he said, then added without irony, "I can't betray that confidence."

Melissa considered this. "Right," she said. "Anyway, this week has been a little stressful. But I'm going to continue talking with Paige, and hopefully I'll understand all of this a little better."

Melissa stood to leave and said, "I need to get back to work. Big deadline looming."

"Alright," he said. "Listen, Melissa, don't stress out. These things tend to work themselves out. And you're not the only one going through this. If you need to talk, drop by my office. My lips are sealed."

"Will do, Doug. See ya." She left the break room.

Doug considered their conversation. Apparently Abby and Melissa, two people who couldn't be more different if they tried, had more or less arrived at a similar conclusion. This report was somewhat painful, but it could also be helpful. Still, their supposed issues didn't involve character. He felt like people were saying, even unintentionally, that he was flawed as a person. And how could you change that?

■　　■　　■

JIM TRUSSEL knocked on the doorframe to Doug's office.

"Hey, Doug," Jim said, "is now a good time?"

Doug looked up from his computer monitor and waved him in. "Jim, my door is always open to you."

Jim smiled and walked into the office. "I don't need much of your time. I just need to provide authorization on Stacy's family leave request for next month."

"Right, right," Doug said. "Let me just locate it," he said, rifling through the inbox on his desk. "Here we go."

Doug opened the file folder and flipped the approval form around so Jim could sign it.

"Got a pen?" Jim asked.

"But of course," Doug said, handing him a pen.

Jim scribbled out his signature and handed back the pen.

"How's everything going?" Doug asked.

"Good, good," Jim said, not entirely convincing. "Just staying busy."

"I hear that," Doug said. He dropped his voice and said, "This 360 thing is keeping everyone busy."

Jim furrowed his brow and said, "Really?"

"Yeah, causing a stir around the office."

Curiosity overcame Jim's better judgment and he asked, "What have you heard?"

"Just that everyone is kind of shocked by the whole experience," Doug replied. He added, "Even Abby."

"Really," Jim mumbled.

"I mean, she's coming to terms with it, I think. But she's not thrilled by it, either."

Jim didn't reply. Doug knew that unlike Vegas, what happened in Doug's office had no chance of staying there.

"Melissa's had some problems, too," Doug said. "She's taking it pretty rough."

Jim nodded but again didn't reply.

Doug realized that Jim wasn't going to comment or offer any insight on his own 360 report, so Doug said, "Anyway, just what you would expect, right? No one enjoys being criticized for their short-comings. Or, in this case, their *perceived* shortcomings."

"That's true," Jim replied. He stood to go and said, "Well, thanks again for letting me interrupt your day."

DOUG knocked on Penny Boykin's open door. Penny looked and up and smiled.

"Hi, Doug," she said warmly, setting down her pen. "How are you?"

"I'm okay," he replied. "Got a minute?"

"Sure," Penny said.

Doug sat down and asked, "How are you doing?

"I'm fine. Well," she laughed, "maybe not fine. I have only two days to meet a crazy deadline. So let me revise that by saying I'm stressed, but it's all good."

"Can you be both?" Doug smiled.

"Sure," Penny replied. "I just compartmentalize. Business over here, personal over there."

What if they're overlapping? "That's a healthy approach." He paused and then said, "Honestly, this 360 thing is heavy."

Penny nodded.

"I know this hasn't been an easy process for anyone," he continued. "But mine feels a little more personal."

"How so?" Penny asked.

"Well, I scored fine in most areas," Doug said. "But one section was pretty rough. People seem to think I'm not confidential."

"Really?" Penny asked, yet not entirely surprised.

"Yeah," he said. "And the low scores were bad enough. Then you have the comments. People said I share personal information about employees. No, *inappropriately* share information."

Penny nodded slightly.

"Saying I'm untrustworthy is a lot different than saying that I need to work on building talent," Doug said. "Or that I need to increase my knowledge. Or even professionalism. Saying someone is untrustworthy is like saying they have a character flaw.

"I mean, it's tough being in HR," he continued. "Relationships are my job. So I end up hearing a lot of information, most of it confidential.

But it's not like I go around doing character assassinations. It's just part of the office environment, you know? I'm not doing anything differently than other people."

Penny considered her reply and then said, "I understand. But I don't think that people are saying you have a flawed character. I know that you have people's best interests in mind."

"I don't know," Doug said, "it doesn't sound that way. Some of the comments were pretty harsh."

"Have you met with Paige yet?" Penny asked. "I'm sure she would have more insight into this than I do."

Doug glanced at Penny's wall clock. "Actually, I meet with her in five minutes. So I'd better go." He stood to leave. "Thanks for listening, Penny. I appreciate it."

Doug made his way to his office, wondering if he should cancel and schedule a root canal.

■   ■   ■

PAIGE was waiting by Doug's office when he returned.

"Hi, Doug," she said, extending her hand. "I'm early."

"No problem, Paige," he said, shaking her hand and not looking at her. "Let's just get started."

They entered Doug's office and he took a seat at his desk while she sat opposite him.

"So how are you?" she asked with genuine concern.

"Fine." He thought a moment and said, "Okay, not fine." Doug slid the 360 report across his desk and opened it. "I'm still kind of reeling from my report."

"Okay," Paige nodded. "What are your thoughts?"

"Well, I did well in some areas," he replied. "A few actually."

"You did," she said. "Knowledgeable. Building Talent. Execution. Really outstanding, Doug."

"I guess," he said. "But this one section pretty much invalidates everything else. People don't think I'm trustworthy. That's a major blow and seems way worse than the other categories."

"Why is that?" Paige asked.

"Because you can develop the other areas. You can become more professional, or more knowledgeable, or even develop your leadership skills. But Trustworthiness seems like an inherent trait, you know? Like people are criticizing your character. That's crushing."

"I understand," Paige nodded. "We can talk about it. But why don't we start from square one and go from there? It will help to better understand how this can help."

Doug nodded. "Okay."

"First," she began, "this assessment is for your benefit. I know that's a little tough to believe at the beginning. But I have done this assessment with all kinds of businesses and teams. And I can tell you that it is beneficial for people in the long run."

Doug smiled weakly. "And the short run?"

She smiled. "It can be tough to hear. Anytime we hear something remotely critical, we cringe. But we can't really grow unless we are able to acknowledge our challenges, especially our blind spots. The 360 removes any blind spots we may have."

Doug nodded.

"Second," she continued. "Think of the positive scores and comments you received. That would seem to indicate that people think you're doing your job, right?"

"I guess so," Doug hesitantly agreed.

"Now, if people flat-out disliked you, or wanted to hurt you, they would just give you low scores across the board. But they didn't. Which tells me that, not only do you do a good job, but you're well-liked, too."

Doug slowly nodded. "Okay."

"Third," she said, "untrustworthy doesn't necessarily mean you have bad character. Remember, they like you. So they probably don't think you're a bad person. In this case, they're referring to what you *do*, not who you *are*."

Doug again nodded and said, "Okay."

"Considering all of that," Paige said, "can you see where they're coming from?"

Doug paused and then said reluctantly, "I guess so. The comments mostly said that I share personal information about other people. But that's just the usual water cooler talk. Everyone does it. Why am I being singled out?"

"Let's say, for argument's sake, that most people do vent their frustrations about their teammates with other people. Or disclose some personal or inappropriate information. " Paige said. "But you're the head of HR. People confide in you. You're privy to a lot of personal information. So because of your role, people do hold you to a higher standard when it comes to sharing company information."

Doug nodded slightly.

"People expect you to be above the fray," Paige said. "To rise above what may be accepted from others. That may sound strange, but I would say that's actually a compliment. They expect more, not less, discretion and professionalism from you."

Doug considered a moment and said, "Okay. That makes sense."

Paige smiled. "Good."

"Honestly," Doug said, "I had no expectation that this meeting would change things. But, I admit, you've definitely given me a different perspective."

"Wonderful," Paige exclaimed.

"But I'm still not entirely sure how to even make the right changes, and more importantly, how to gain back people's trust."

"That's okay," Paige smiled. "We're just getting started."

Chapter 7

Professionalism

—noun   *projecting confidence, credibility, and a respect for others*

MARK BROCKETT leaned to the side and shifted his computer bag to a more secure position on his shoulder. One hand gripped a muffin, while the other hand had two fingers trapping his cell phone against a Styrofoam coffee cup. The elevator dinged and he exited through the sliding doors. The computer bag continued to slide against his will, prompting Mark to compensate by leaning to the side as he shuffled to his office.

Mark opened his office door and set the muffin on the desk while letting his computer bag slip off his arm onto the floor. He rounded the desk and plopped down into his executive chair. He turned on his two computers and three monitors. Mark unwrapped the muffin, propped his feet up on the hutch, and took a big bite.

Everything seemed business as usual; another typical start to a typical workday. But Mark understood that things had changed. Last week he was the go-to guy for all things technical at Collier, the foremost and—he believed—respected authority on computers, networking, and, most crucially it seemed, hand held electronic devices. He and his team kept the technological wheels turning each day.

That was before his 360 assessment. The report drew a dividing line on his career at Collier. Before the report, he knew that he did an outstanding job. After the 360, his performance seemed overshadowed by the report's critique of his professional standards.

Mark had never received direct complaints about his appearance, humor, or personal style. Maybe a stray comment from Larry or another executive, but those seemed more like lighthearted jokes than serious critiques. And nothing as direct as the 360.

Mark found it difficult to believe that being exceptional at his job wasn't enough. *Do I need to start reading GQ? Do I need a personal shopper? A valet named Jeeves?* Were these issues really pertinent to his job?

The morning sun streamed in through Mark's smudged and streaked window. He had never taken notice.

■   ■   ■

KYLE CONNICK peered around Mark's open door.

"Mark, what's up?"

Mark looked up from his computer monitor and smiled. "Hey, Kyle. Just getting started on the day."

Kyle was an analyst on Mark's team and a friend outside the office. In fact, Mark was friendly and casual with most of his subordinates, a trait that endeared him to the team but sometimes made him seem less than authoritative.

Kyle walked in and found a spot on the floor that was free of papers and files. He leaned against the wall and said, "So, a bunch of us are heading to Dale's tonight for the big game. You in?"

Mark thoughtfully sipped his coffee and replied, "I don't know. I have a late-afternoon meeting with Paige and I'm not sure how long it will run."

Kyle raised his eyebrows. "The assessment coach? I thought all of that was over and done with."

"No," Mark smiled thinly. "Turns out it's just getting started."

Mark's phone buzzed and he picked up the receiver. "Hey, Larry."

Kyle tuned out Mark's conversation and casually surveyed the office. Everywhere he looked were stacks of papers and files. Even Mark's loveseat and coffee table held reports.

To Kyle's left was a wall of shelving that held hundreds of computer parts and components. The wall facing Mark held more shelving that contained hundreds of manuals. The right wall was dominated by a large but greasy picture window.

There seemed no clear rhyme or reason to the chaos, but Mark's sloppiness in manner and appearance was generally tolerated because of his sheer brilliance. He also understood every nuance and aspect of everyone's job on his team. Finally, Mark was a nice guy and actually pretty attractive, albeit unpolished in more ways than one.

Mark placed the phone on the cradle. "Sorry about that. Gotta run by Larry's office in a few minutes." Mark wadded up his muffin wrapper and tossed it at the wastebasket. The wrapper bounced off the wall and into the basket, although, Kyle noted, it wouldn't make much difference if it joined the paper on the floor.

"Anyway. Tonight. Put me down as a tentative yes," Mark said. He leaned back and said. "First the report. Now meetings with the consultant. This 360 has been an experience."

"It's certainly different," Kyle replied, unable to hide his discomfort. He had been selected to participate on Mark's assessment.

While his ratings and comments were generally very favorable, Kyle had noted some areas where Mark could improve. And, according to office chatter, Kyle's viewpoints were in line with the majority.

Mark broke the awkward silence and said, "Anyway, I'll catch up with you later."

"Good deal," Kyle said, thankful for his easy out.

As Kyle returned to his desk, he reflected on his own assessment of Mark. He had given Mark high scores for Knowledge (which was off the chart), Trustworthiness (he was always fair and forthcoming with his team and, seemingly, his superiors), and Building Talent (no team member felt unappreciated).

But while Kyle enjoyed the easy camaraderie with his boss, he also understood that Mark's casual manner could be viewed as detrimental to his leadership role. In fact, Kyle often wished that Mark was less of a buddy and more of a boss, trading the chumminess for respect. But what were the odds of Mark making such a big shift?

▧   ▧   ▧

MARK was rummaging through his wall of computer parts when he heard a distinctive voice ring out from the doorway.

"Marky!" Abby said, arriving at his door. "Marky Mark! Are you in here?" she joked, a palm lifted above her eyes, as if trying to locate him in the cluttered room.

Mark forced a laugh. "Hi, Abby. I'm over here by the Wall of 1001 Parts."

"Ah!" she exclaimed. "I was getting worried."

"You know what worry is?"

She smiled. "Sure. When your coworkers can't locate you in your own office." She surveyed the room. "Seriously, Mark, how do you operate in this clutter? I feel disorganized just standing here."

Mark glanced over his shoulder. "It's not clutter. It's a highly complex method for organizing and retrieving information."

Abby laughed. "So complex no one gets it."

"Right. Just give me a sec."

"You can have two," she replied. Abby again took in his chaotic office, frowning at the stacks of paper, with her eyes finally resting on Mark as he searched through his shelves, appraising his appearance. *This man needs an extreme makeover.*

If Abby was a paragon of fashion, Mark was a study in what-not-to-wear even though he was a good looking guy. Scuffed boat shoes that were worn out. Baggy gray pants that needed to be pressed. A short-sleeved plaid shirt that was 20 years old. The sum total of his wardrobe was slightly above thrift store. Abby's shoes cost probably more than his entire closet.

Still, Abby mused, Mark wasn't bad looking. He was actually attractive, great hair, still in good shape probably from some college sport that he had told her about but she couldn't remember. Still she couldn't imagine going out with him, being seen outside the office together. Her friends' judgment would be swift. Abby would have to replace his entire wardrobe to make him dateable. And she didn't have time to serve as an image consultant. She had personal development issues on her own plate.

"Okay," Mark said, settling into his chair. "To what do I owe the pleasure of your delightful company?"

She took a seat across from Mark. "As much as I wish this was a social visit, I'm, again, having technical difficulties."

"Plural?" Mark asked.

"Yes. Two, actually."

"Well, let's hear it," he said.

"First, I am still having trouble connecting my laptop to the company network and server when I'm at home. It takes at least 20 minutes. It just makes me crazy to wait."

He nodded. "Okay."

"As a result, I walked into 80+ emails in my inbox this morning."

Mark shrugged. "Didn't you get those emails on your phone?"

"No," she replied. "That's number two. I'm also having trouble getting my phone to connect to our email server." She smiled. "Is the IT department plotting against me, Mark?"

"We're certainly more creative than that," Mark said with some embarrassment.

"Wonderful. Then please apply that marvelous creativity to making my technical life work."

Mark leaned forward on his elbows. "If you don't mind parting with your cell for a few minutes, I'll have someone look at it now," he said.

Abby held out the device then snatched it back from his grasp. "You do know this is my most important accessory, right?"

"More than your $500 shoes?"

"Believe it or not, yes. Sometimes function trumps form. Rarely, but it can happen."

"Right," Mark said.

She handed him her phone. "Please make haste," she said, rising to leave. "My world will stop revolving until I get it back."

Mark smiled. "What should I do if your boyfriend calls?"

Abby blushed but replied, "I don't have time for boyfriends right now. I barely have time for me."

■   ■   ■

MARK rapped his knuckles on Larry's office door. Larry, on the phone, waved him in.

Mark walked into Larry's office and, as always, enjoyed the stunning panorama of the beachside. The view was definitely great at the top.

Larry hung up the phone and said, "Hey, Mark, have a seat," waving to a chair in front of his desk.

Larry considered Mark a moment and said, "How's everything going?"

"Good," Mark replied. "We're focusing on some security upgrades this weekend. But it's business as usual."

"Good, good," Larry said. He paused and then continued, "Listen, this may sound unusual. But I want to bring something to your attention."

Mark shifted in his seat. "Okay."

"I know you've been corresponding with some vendors about new hardware. You've copied me on those emails, of course."

Mark nodded.

"But here's the thing," Larry said. "Some of these emails—actually, most of them—tend to be, well, less than professional in tone."

Mark didn't reply.

"I know that you have some degree of relationship with these people, and I appreciate that. But, when we're discussing business issues with individuals outside the company, it's vital that we maintain a professional image. And part of maintaining that image is communication. Right?"

Mark nodded. "Of course."

"Business-related emails need to be professional in tone," Larry continued. "In fact, any email that has Collier's name in it represents our company. So if a Collier email contains jokes—whether appropriate to the other person or not—or flippant asides or comments, I see it as a reflection on our company. Would you agree?"

"Absolutely."

Larry seemed uncomfortable with the topic but pressed on. "You've also made disparaging comments about vendors. Granted, we no longer use those vendors, but it still doesn't reflect well on the company and, honestly, yourself."

Mark took a breath and nodded.

"Look, Mark," Larry said, in a softer tone. "You're an essential part of my team. Know that. I'm telling you this because I believe that by addressing this issue, you could enhance your stature, both inside and outside the company."

Larry thought a moment and said, "We've all had our share of challenges this week. This 360 thing hasn't been easy for anyone, myself included. So don't feel that I'm singling you out. But I'm willing to bet I'm not the only who sees this, right?"

Mark cleared his throat. "A few people mentioned it in my 360 report."

Larry nodded. "Mark, this is an easy fix. I'm asking you to make sure that any business-related emails or forwards are professional in tone and content. Okay? And then we move on."

■   ■   ■

DOUG LAPAR walked into the break room and found Mark sitting at a table, reading a trade magazine and nursing a coffee.

"Hey, Mark, how's it going?'

Doug looked up. "Not great, Doug."

"Really?" Doug asked, taking a seat opposite Mark. "Let me guess. The 360 report."

Mark considered several replies, but said "Pretty much."

"Listen," Doug said, leaning forward. "Don't take it too tough. Everybody's having issues with the report."

"Really?"

"Yeah," Doug said, dropping his voice lower. "More than a few people are struggling with their scores, especially the comments."

Mark nodded.

"People like Melissa. Abby." Doug paused then spread his arms and said, "Even me."

Mark smiled. "Wow, even you."

"I know, right," Doug laughed. He thought and then said, "But here's the thing. The report is here. We have to deal with it. So maybe resistance is futile." He laughed again.

"Maybe," Mark said. "But some of these issues, I'm not sure how to even begin addressing them."

▓   ▓   ▓

PAIGE peered into Mark's office. "Hey, Mark, are you ready for me?"

Mark looked up from his monitor. "Sure. Come in and have a seat wherever there's space."

Paige chuckled. "I can do that." She took a seat across from him. "How are you?"

"Good," Mark replied, then reconsidered. "Okay, that's a stock answer. Actually, not so good."

"Okay."

"As you can imagine," Mark began, "The 360 report has definitely made an impact on me."

Paige nodded.

"Honestly, I kind of knew some of these issues, in a very peripheral, subconscious kind of way. But seeing them on paper, and having your colleagues make these statements, is an experience."

"I understand," Paige said. "What are your thoughts about their feedback?"

"I don't really know yet," Mark said, picking up his report. "I scored well in a few areas, like Knowledge, Innovation, and Building Talent. So that's easy enough to take. But my scores and comments under Professionalism pretty much made those accolades pale by comparison."

"Mark, you did well in most areas," Paige said. "And those other comments in no way invalidate your accolades. You are universally considered one of the most knowledgeable and innovative people on Larry's team. Those areas are absolutely critical to your role here, and necessary to get Collier to the next level."

Mark slightly nodded.

"It's never easy for anyone to hear criticism," Paige continued. "Even criticism that is offered with the best of intentions. Yet the 360 is exactly that: critiques that have your best interests at heart."

Mark again nodded.

"Yes," Paige said, "but you also need to enjoy the accolades because the positive feedback is just as important."

"Okay. Maybe." He picked up his report. "So, let's see. Professionalism. A few comments said that my appearance is too casual. Which I get, but I don't."

"Okay."

"I'm not like Abby, who has to meet with clients all day," he said. "I'm not trying to sell anything. I provide services, almost entirely in-house. And when I do interact with vendors, it's almost always through email. So who cares if I'm not wearing a three thousand-dollar suit? What's the point? I'm not trying to impress my team."

"I get that," Paige said. "But our appearance isn't always about impressing people. It conveys other messages. For example, if you see someone in a well-tailored suit, you form a general impression about them, right? You might think credible, confident, and probably professional."

"I guess."

"Think of it as making a positive non-verbal statement. Wearing the right clothes can convey authority to your team and peers. It can provide you with immediate credibility."

Mark laughed. "Really?"

Paige smiled. "In a perfect world, we would be judged strictly on our ability, not by first impressions or appearances. But reality is different. People are going to form impressions and attitudes based on how we present ourselves. And for better or worse, clothing and personal style are a part of that."

"I guess," Mark said. He glanced down at the report. "Apparently I'm too casual all around."

"The good news, Mark, is that you can take steps to address these issues and it gets noticed right away."

Mark nodded. "People also believe I don't always communicate in a professional way. Larry actually talked about this with me today. He said I need to keep any work emails strictly professional."

"Do you agree?" Paige asked.

"I mean, yeah. Sort of." Mark considered. "I was just trying to keep things light with our suppliers, you know? Just some fun jokes, a little political humor, and comments. It was all harmless."

"Right," Paige nodded. "And I'm sure your jokes *were* harmless. The problem comes down to perspective. What's appropriate to one person may be inappropriate to someone else. So instead of continually gauging what's appropriate with different people, it's easier and safer to err on the side of staying professional. Friendly, but professional. Less fun, maybe, but it prevents miscommunication and unwanted forwards."

Mark nodded.

"Also," Paige continued, "just as with our image, every email, phone call, including our LinkedIn and Facebook pages reflect on us. For you, email may be the most important, because, using email, you interact with people whom you've never even met. When you're just corresponding electronically, that's your only way to make a good impression."

Mark again nodded.

"Okay," Mark said and thought a moment. "Still not entirely sold. But this meeting wasn't as scary as I imagined."

"Don't be surprised. And the process will become even less scary."

"That would be good."

Chapter 8

Execution

—noun   *taking action on key priorities and making timely decisions*

PENNY BOYKIN trudged into her kitchen. She glanced at the microwave clock. 8:14 a.m. Penny was going to be late. But then, she had practically lived at the office for the past 48 hours. She poured a mug of coffee as her husband entered the kitchen, back from his morning run.

"Good morning," he said, chipper, wide-awake, ready to take on the world. Randy King, a military systems consultant, had been a U.S. Naval officer for 20 years. It was during a tour of duty in Japan that Randy met and began dating Penny, then a college student at the University of Tokyo. It was a whirlwind courtship that resulted in marriage just a year later.

They were a solid couple, each bringing different strengths to the relationship. Randy was disciplined, structured, and enjoyed routine. Penny was bright, highly educated, and thrived on variety. While they both were early risers, Penny wasn't thrilled to greet this particular morning.

Randy grabbed a bottled water from the fridge. "Late night, huh?"

"Yes. Early morning, actually." Penny slid into a chair at the table.

"Get everything done?" Randy sat down across from her.

"Barely," she replied, sipping her coffee. "Taylor kind of dropped the ball, so I had to do some pinch-hitting."

Randy nodded. Taylor Jennings was the financial director at Collier. Randy knew that the work in question was a collection of financial projections for next year.

"So why didn't Taylor stay and finish the reports?" Randy asked.

"I don't know," Penny said, stifling a yawn. "I'm ultimately responsible for all of the financial reports, so I just decided to do it myself. And honestly, I probably had Taylor working on too many other projects."

Penny looked into her mug and added, "And staying busy kept me from having to deal with that 360 report."

"Oh, really," Randy said, raising his eyebrows. "You got your feedback?"

"Earlier this week," she replied. "I've wanted to talk with you about it, but I've been so preoccupied with getting these reports finished, I could barely schedule sleep."

"Okay," Randy nodded. "Tonight?"

"Tonight," she said, rising from her chair. "But first, I need to make it through today," as she gave him a quick squeeze.

■　　■　　■

PENNY strode quickly through the lobby. She glanced at her watch. 9:30. Larry was probably looking for her. She stepped through the elevator doors and pressed the button for her floor.

Alone in the elevator, Penny was able to indulge in a last-minute appearance check in the elevator's mirrored doors. Her shoulder-length dark hair was, as usual, smartly pulled into a French twist. Her black jacket and skirt were the perfect cut and fit for her small frame. Pearl earrings with a strand of freshwater pearls around her neck, a tasteful watch, and her pave diamond wedding band completed the look. Penny brushed a stray hair off of her shoulder. While she wasn't preoccupied with designer labels like Abby, Penny always maintained a polished, sharp appearance. *Who can even see the label, anyway?*

Penny stepped off of the elevator and walked toward her office, greeting other employees as she moved through the hallway. She unlocked her office door, flipped on the lights, and stepped inside. *This place looks familiar.*

As she waited for her computer to boot up, Penny dialed up her voicemail. As she had suspected, Larry was indeed looking for her. His voice floated up from the speakerphone.

"Morning, Penny. So I'm looking at your reports, and judging by the timestamp, it looks like you or someone on your team had a late night. Thanks for getting these done. When you have a chance, swing by my office."

Penny pressed 'end' and sat back in her chair. She glanced at the monitor, the computer still starting up. Email or Larry? Penny stood and left her office.

≋   ≋   ≋

PENNY approached the desk of Larry's assistant, Natalie.

"Penny!" Larry boomed from his office. "Come on in."

"I think he's ready for you," Natalie smiled.

"Good morning, Penny," Larry said as she walked into the office. "Or is it evening for you?" He smiled.

She laughed. "It's all starting to blend into one, endless day."

Larry moved from behind his desk and indicated the sofa and loveseat. Penny sat on the loveseat while Larry chose a wingback chair.

"Thank you again for the report," he said. "It's already in Greg's hands."

"You're welcome, Larry."

"I don't tell you enough, Penny, but you are a rock to me," Larry continued. "To Collier. All of your hard work is appreciated."

Penny nodded. "Thank you so much for saying so."

Larry thought a moment and then said, "I am concerned about one thing, though."

"And what's that?" she asked, concern underlining the words.

"I mentioned this in my voicemail. The timestamp on the report was after three in the morning. Are we not giving your team enough time to complete these reports during business hours?"

"No." She corrected herself, "I mean yes, you are. It's not that. The deadlines are fine. I just got sidetracked by other projects."

"Okay." He nodded thoughtfully. "But, this isn't the first time you've pulled an all-nighter. It seems to be a regular hazard of your job."

Penny smiled nervously. "I guess I just tend to work that way. An approaching deadline seems to give me more focus and drive. I feel like I perform best when the clock is ticking and I'm feeling the pressure."

Larry again nodded. "Well, I can't complain about your work. Your reports are always practically flawless. But it seems to me that you may be killing yourself to get it done."

"Thanks, Larry. I'll try to refine my approach going forward."

"Right," Larry smiled as he stood. "Let's aim for 2:00 a.m. next time."

■   ■   ■

TAYLOR JENNINGS knocked on Penny's open office door. "Hey, Penny, got a minute?"

"Sure, Taylor," Penny said, looking up from a report. "Come in. Have a seat. How's it going?"

"It's going well," he replied. "I just wanted to apologize again for not finishing that report yesterday."

"It's fine," she said. "I knocked it out last night. The important thing now is that it's done."

"Okay," he nodded. "It's just that…I really don't want to make excuses, but those last-minute cost analysis reports kept me pretty busy. I hadn't really factored those into my schedule."

"I understand," Penny said, not really having a strong reply. "I'll try to better prioritize projects going forward."

"Alright," Taylor said, rising to leave. "Thanks for understanding."

"Anytime," Penny said, watching him leave. And she did understand. More than that, she was beginning to understand how her unorthodox work habits were affecting the team.

▦   ▦   ▦

PAIGE rapped on Penny's doorframe.

"Hi, Penny," she said. "Are you ready?"

Penny looked up from her computer monitor. "Schedule-wise, sure. Personally? Maybe not. But come on in."

Paige walked into the office and glanced around. Penny's office décor reflected an international sensibility. Delicate Asian pieces mingled with bronze sculptures, showcasing a broad appreciation for eras and artists.

The office, Paige thought, reflected Penny's global background that probably resulted from a nomadic military life. Paige knew that Penny's international worldview was influenced by both her place of birth and her husband's many assignments. This served Penny well, as Collier was poised to serve global clients.

Paige admired Penny's considerable academic degrees, collected from fine schools both overseas and in the states. Penny was no doubt exceptionally bright. But even the brightest people were susceptible to personal and professional blind spots.

Penny swiveled her chair away from the monitor and smiled graciously. "Please have a seat."

Paige sat opposite Penny and said, "I love your office. I could spend a few hours here just taking everything in."

Penny smiled. "Thank you. I've certainly been lucky to live and travel to some amazing places around the world."

"That's fantastic." Paige settled in her chair. "So, how are you?"

"Well. Busy." Penny paused. "Concerned."

"Concerned?" Paige asked.

Penny retrieved her 360 from the hutch. She opened the report on her desk and flipped through the pages.

"Yes, concerned. Very much so, actually."

Paige nodded. "Before we get to your concerns, let's talk about other areas of the report. Your peers consider you outstanding in Professionalism, Character, and Knowledge. You actually did very well overall. So well, in fact, that your area of opportunity is relatively narrow."

Penny offered a slight smile. "That's certainly a positive way to say 'Needs Improvement.'"

■　　■　　■

PENNY and Paige sat next to each other as they viewed the 360 report on the desk.

"Let's start with a comment," Paige suggested.

"Okay," Penny sighed. She scanned the page and read aloud, "'Penny often waits until the last minute to initiate reporting assignments among the team. As a result, team members scramble to complete reports within a very narrow time frame.'"

"What are your thoughts on that comment?" Paige asked.

"I can see that," Penny admitted. "I've been thinking about it ever since I got my 360. It's not so much about procrastination, I think. I'm often sidetracked by other projects and reports. These side jobs tend to take up time that could be spent compiling reports."

Paige nodded.

"I'm very deadline-driven," Penny continued. "Initially it may seem like I have enough time to do every project I can imagine. It's only when that deadline is bearing down on me that reality sinks in. By that time, everyone on the team—myself included—is frantically trying to fit a week into 48 hours."

"As we move forward," Paige said, "We'll seek ways to bring a better sense of balance and priority to your reporting schedules. There is urgent and then there is important. We'll look at both."

Penny nodded. "I think, too, that I can often go after what's interesting instead of focusing on the work at hand. I enjoy finance, of course. Yet the bread-and-butter reports can sometimes feel mundane. Finance isn't necessarily glamorous or fun, but I'm intrigued by projects that veer from the routine. So I would have to say that a desire for variety fuels this issue, too."

"That makes sense," Paige observed. "We all need some degree of variety in our work, no matter what the section or field. We can certainly find ways to both enhance your primary role and supplement your need for a bit of professional adventure."

"I like that." Penny smiled and said, "You know, this is a little less painful that I thought."

"I'm so glad to hear that," Paige enthused.

Penny turned back to her report. True, this experience was proving less traumatic than she had previously thought. But there was still a nagging issue in her mind that she wasn't ready to share with Paige.

PENNY exited the parking garage and began to navigate the afternoon commuting traffic. After her meeting with Paige, Penny decided to leave early and try to relax this evening. She was pleased to find that traffic was relatively light at this hour on the freeway.

Penny placed the car on cruise control and allowed her mind to wander. Penny's meeting with Paige left her feeling somewhat more encouraged.

It wasn't pleasant to hear critiques from anyone, especially those she most admired and trusted. Yet she realized that no one was perfect at all aspects of their job. And she was self-aware enough to know that she probably had discovered some professional blind spots. Sore spots, too, she thought wryly.

Still, there were some issues she wasn't ready to address at the office. Maybe she could first find some perspective at home.

▪   ▪   ▪

RANDY was typing an email in his home office when he heard the garage door open. He quickly finished the email, clicked 'send,' and went to meet Penny in the kitchen.

Penny walked through the garage entrance into the kitchen and met Randy as he walked in.

"Hi," she said, giving Randy a kiss. "I decided to cut out early."

"Wonderful," Randy replied. "Does this mean I can play hooky, too?"

"Oh, yes," Penny said, dropping her computer back onto a kitchen chair. "But just from your current job. Instead of consulting, I need you to switch gears and play psychologist."

Randy smiled. "I can do that. And, as a key part of my recommended therapy, I always include comfort food."

▪   ▪   ▪

PENNY and Randy sat at the kitchen table, a nearly-empty pizza box resting between them on the table. Penny had let her hair down, literally, and changed into jeans and a t-shirt. The conversation had centered on small talk, each just enjoying an early evening together. Randy knew Penny would talk when she was ready.

Penny toyed with the pizza crust on her paper plate and said, "So, reports are a big part of my job. And I have yet to meet one I couldn't tackle. But this 360 report has proved the exception."

Randy sipped his soda and nodded encouragingly.

"It's not so much the contents of the report," she continued. "I can see how certain habits of mine could affect the team.

"The scales and numbers are mostly helpful, but the negative written comments are hard to read."

"Sure," Randy agreed.

Penny leaned back in her chair and sighed. "But it's more than just the report," she said. "Now that I've seen these comments, I'm beginning to look at my team and environment in a different way. To see issues and events differently than I have in the past."

She considered a moment and then said, "And what I'm really afraid of is that these issues have directly caused people to leave my team and Collier."

Randy leaned forward on the table. "Now Penny, I don't know if you should take it that far. Those people left for other opportunities."

"Sort of," Penny said. "But remember Lateshia and Kenneth?" Randy nodded, recognizing former members from Penny's team. "They really struggled to meet deadlines. And they had each confided in some team members, who then shared it with me, that they were reeling under the time-sensitive pressure in our department. Our work can be high pressure, no doubt. But no one should have struggled as much as they did. Lateshia has two young kids and Kenneth had a 2 hour commute."

"So maybe they weren't right for the job," Randy suggested.

"No," Penny said, shaking her head. "They were both extremely bright and hard-working. They understood Collier's financials at every level. Looking back, it seems that they just couldn't accommodate my urgent, last minute deadlines."

Randy smiled.

"I do realize that while I may find it stimulating and exciting to have a last minute deadline, other people find it terribly stressful. They want more structure and predictability and they don't thrive on constant change and pressure." She added with a new level of self-awareness, "So maybe they just don't want to be gluttons for punishment and get 3 hours of sleep a night."

"It can't be that bad," Randy observed. "Your turnover rate isn't that high."

"I know," Penny said. "But still, both of those people were great employees and added value to my team. Maybe they did leave for a better opportunity, but I know they loved Collier and what we're doing. The country, the world, is on the verge of the next big wave of energy solutions and we're right at the forefront. They knew that. And they believed in what we are doing. So I naturally wonder why two people who so believed in Collier would leave for supposedly greener pastures." She smiled. "No pun intended."

"Okay," Randy nodded. "So let's say your leadership style doesn't work for everyone. Results still matter. And let's not forget, you get results. So much so, that Larry thinks the world of you."

"He does value my contribution," Penny agreed. "He even told me so today."

"See," Randy said. "That should be encouraging."

"It is," she said, then paused. "But I still need to take an honest look at how I'm running my team. How I may be helping or hurting their work. And maybe most importantly, how I'm encouraging or discouraging them."

"Sounds like you realize the problem," Randy said. "So how do you find the solution?"

Penny stood and picked up the pizza box. "That is the question. Paige told me today that this meeting was just the beginning. If so, I guess the answers should unfold during the next few weeks. One thing I do know for sure."

"Oh yeah?" Randy said, beginning to clear the table.

"There's no way the next few weeks can top this one."

Chapter 9

Larry and Paige

PAIGE walked through the club entrance and was greeted by the maitre'de.

"Hello," Paige said. "I'm meeting Larry Wesley."

The host nodded and crisply replied, "Please, follow me."

As Paige walked to the table she took in the plush surroundings. Dark, lustrous woods. Polished brass rails. Burgundy leather seating offering a contrast to the starched white table linens. Plush carpet that whispered as she moved across the floor.

Masculine. Classic. Clubby. Yes, this was exactly where she would have pictured Larry Wesley dining. All that was missing were silver haired men nursing cigars while reading *The Economist*.

Paige approached Larry's table and he rose to greet her.

"Hello, Paige," Larry greeted her.

"Hi, Larry," she said, smiling as she shook his hand. The host pulled out a chair and she took a seat. "Thank you for making time to meet with me."

"No problem," Larry smiled thinly. "Thanks for meeting me here. I needed a break from the office."

"Of course." Paige detected a slight thawing in his attitude toward her. While he wouldn't change overnight, Larry was slowly coming around to the idea that Paige was not the enemy, and the 360 was not a professional bomb. Slowly.

Paige again surveyed the dimly lit room and said, "Nice place."

"Predictable, right?" Larry smirked.

Paige laughed. "I like it."

"So," Larry said, "how goes the coaching?"

"Very well. You really have a tremendous team."

"I do," Larry nodded. "Or is it *did*? Are they all staying on after the 360?"

Paige laughed. "Yes. They're all very dedicated to the company and to you as their leader."

"Right." He remarked with a little irony, "My assessment certainly reflected their dedication to providing me feedback."

"They truly do admire you. The 360 comments aren't about a breach in loyalty." She added teasingly, "No one is perfect, Larry. Not even you."

Larry laced his fingers in front of him and said, "I know I'm not flawless. I can come across as arrogant. I take charge. I get things done, even if that steps on some people's toes. I can come across as elitist." He waved an arm, sweeping the room. "I even dine in elitist clubs.

"But it's alarming to hear these critiques from my own leadership team. I feel like I do everything possible to empower and encourage them in their roles. Yet we have some problems. So how can I begin to repair the fractures that may be spreading throughout the team? Between myself and them?"

"Well, Larry, I have one suggestion."

＊　　＊　　＊

PAIGE sat in the Collier conference room, her chair hugging a wall near the head of the table. She thought back to her first meeting with the leadership team in this room. While those people still seemed a bit on edge, she was greeted by each person who entered the room, each displaying a unique mix of familiarity, warmth, and caution. She was their advocate but didn't really fall into any specific job description within the company.

Paige was like an exchange student, striving to understand the nuances and language of her environment and culture, within a shorter and more temporary timeline than her peers. It's not easy being the new kid in school, she mused.

Larry entered the room and the chatter around the table dropped several decibels, while the temperature in the room seemed to perceptibly drop several degrees. He briefly acknowledged his team with a nod and then continued to absently thumb through a report.

Larry took fleeting glances at everyone sitting around the table. On a rational level, Larry understood that no one sitting in the room harbored any ill will against him. And while Larry somewhat realized that he was primarily struggling with his wounded pride, he was not always the forgiving or forgetting type. Everyone here clearly understood that.

Larry placed the report on the table and looked directly at the group. The room immediately became still.

"Good morning, everyone," he began. "I appreciate everyone being here."

Larry paused a moment, considering his words. His better self needed to show up.

"First, I want to thank and commend you all for working through what has been a difficult few weeks. This assessment period has been challenging. For me, at least.

"The 360 reports have recognized our many collective and personal strengths. Our dedication to professional standards, behaviors, and attitudes. Our desire to build strong teams. Our considerable knowledge of a complex, fledgling, and soon to be thriving industry. Our ability to execute plans and ideas that will build this company."

He again paused and then continued. "But the report has also unearthed some personal and professional blind spots. You may believe that these issues should have been best left buried beneath the surface of our group." He glanced at Paige. "I myself am still working out in my own mind how to make this feedback positively impact what we do and how we do it.

"Regardless, the issues are now laid out in black and white. Greg is committed to our addressing these issues, and I in turn am committed to this course of action. So while I recognize, and even sympathize, with your attitudes and responses to the 360, I also encourage each of you to approach this assessment period with an open mind."

Larry glanced around the table and said. "These reports are personal, there's no doubt of that. Each section addresses our specific strengths and weaknesses in our current roles. But while the comments are personal, the results affect the entire team.

"After speaking with several of you, I realize that—left unaddressed—our reactions and responses to the 360 report have the potential to fragment our incredible group. And the health of this team is more vital to our success than the launch of any plan, proposal, or product. Going forward, this team's health is our collective first priority."

Larry indicated Paige and said, "Considering that, Paige has suggested, and I agreed, that she join us on our annual leadership retreat. In fact, we're including an extra day, so Paige can facilitate a leadership workshop."

The group collectively shifted in their chairs.

"I realize that everyone here has a tremendous amount of work in the pipeline. There's never a shortage. Yet in spite of those demands, I think that this group retreat is even more vital to our continued and future success. We must address these issues personally and collectively to preserve our group dynamic. How we work together. And how we support each other. This is tantamount to Collier's future growth." *And probably to me keeping my job.*

Chapter 10

A Journey to the Retreat

JIM SROKA pinned his newspaper and book under his arm, placed his computer bag into the overhead compartment, and slid into the leather window seat. Buckling his seatbelt, Jim gazed through the small window at the bustling activity of baggage handlers roaming the tarmac. In a few moments they would be airborne and cruising toward Utah. Jim was more than ready to arrive.

He stuffed his book into the rear seat pouch and opened his *Wall Street Journal*. Jim idly glanced through the pages and considered the trip's itinerary. While the leadership retreat was officially focused on company planning and leadership development, the getaway also offered the team a much-needed break from their very busy lives. Jim believed that business and pleasure were not mutually exclusive.

This particular retreat would be different, however, as Paige was taking an active role in their leadership development sessions.

Though Jim liked Paige, he remained wary of addressing the results from his 360 report. As Jim considered what the next few days would hold, Melissa sat down in the adjoining seat.

"Good morning, Jim," Melissa greeted him.

"That it is," Jim replied. He appraised the reading materials on Melissa's lap: Two heavyweight technical manuals that could only be tremendously boring, Jim thought. His book was a legal thriller, perfect for leisure reading.

"Some light reading, Melissa?"

Melissa smiled and said, "Sure. If you consider 'multijunction photovoltaic cells' light reading."

Jim frowned. "Er, no."

"C'mon. Solar? Light?"

"Oh, right, right," Jim chuckled politely at a pun that only a technophile could appreciate. But the joke also reminded Jim of one big problem. He had no idea what those components referred to.

"So, tell me about these multifunction…" he said casually.

"Multi*junction*," Melissa corrected. "They're part of the third generation of solar cells. They're comprised of thin films that—while more expensive—have proven to be more efficient."

Jim continued to listen as Melissa enthusiastically described Collier's next-generation solar cells and panels. And while he heard every word, he understood about every third sentence. *Not good.*

After she finished Jim commented, "Sounds incredible. I can't wait to see what your team comes up with."

"Definitely." Melissa replied, with more confidence than she felt. In fact, her team had already pitched a number of related ideas, most of which Melissa had soundly rejected. But that was prior to her 360 feedback. She was beginning to listen more closely to her team's recommendations and not cut them off. In fact, she was having one-on-one meetings—scheduled of course—with each of her team with the sole purpose of only asking questions. And not shutting anyone's ideas down. But true to her nature, they got the questions in advance so they could consider their answers.

▨　▨　▨

PENNY BOYKIN took her window seat, two rows behind Jim and Melissa. After another late night at the office, Penny planned on sleeping during the flight. She casually flipped through an in-flight magazine as she waited for the plane to depart.

Though Penny was sitting on the plane, her mind was back at the office. Several board reports were due by Monday and her team was scrambling to make miracles happen, again, in what had become a predictable cycle. But she wasn't there to rescue them, so somehow they would delegate among themselves and figure it out.

Doug LaPar sat down next to Penny, rescuing her from her anxious thoughts.

"Hey Penny," Doug said. "Ready for the trip?"

"Oh yeah," Penny replied. She added wistfully, "I just wish Randy could join me."

Doug nodded, bucking his seatbelt. "Yeah, I know." He lowered his voice and said, "Just part of Larry's unpublished policy regarding spouses and significant others on company trips: his wife, minus every other spouse or partner. You won't find that perk in the Collier Energy handbook."

Penny tactfully dodged this comment and said, "What about you? Ready for a break?"

"Oh, yeah," he said. "I look forward to this trip all year. It's a mental health perk that trumps any corporate benefit." He again lowered his voice and leaned toward her. "And, let me tell you, several people on the team need it."

Penny offered a small smile and returned to her magazine.

Doug folded his arms and closed his eyes. While Penny was always discreet, it occurred to him that maybe it wasn't discretion, but caution, that kept her from sharing her opinions with him. Doug began to wonder if his closest confidant in the office considered him anything but confidential. He began to consider how he could restrain himself and stop talking so much. He had to change the content of his discussions with them before any of the team's perceptions would change.

■   ■   ■

ABBY STRYKER strolled onto the plane with her designer bag in tow. Mark Brockett followed her through the small aisle to their row.

"Mark, could you stow my bag for me?" she asked, already moving into the window seat.

"Uh, sure," Mark said, tugging at the heavy case. "What exactly do you have in here, Abigail?"

"Just my computer, a few books, magazines, a change of shoes, makeup. Everything a girl needs to travel in style and comfort. You understand, right, Mark?"

As Abby watched Mark heft her considerable bag into the overhead compartment, she noted that he, in fact, understood little about style. The retreat's unofficial dress code, business casual, had actually succeeded in doing what Abby thought impossible: It made Mark look even more sloppy than usual.

Mark wore an even older plaid short-sleeve shirt, wrinkled khakis that were too short, no belt, and a pair of worn out loafers with white, ratty socks. Maybe next year he could just roll out of bed and arrive in his pajamas, Abby mused.

In the spirit of Collier's renewable stance, perhaps she should attempt to recycle Mark's current wardrobe and replace it with a more fitting selection of garments. By contrast, she was runway-ready for a business chic fashion show. White, darted Egyptian cotton blouse, tailored trousers, designer jacket, fine jewelry and expensive Italian loafers. Someone has to make us look good, she thought.

Still, behind his messy appearance, Abby recognized that Mark had a lot of potential. She also recognized something more in Mark, which was troubling. Her personal plans had never even considered dating a guy from IT, let alone someone who was completely indifferent to their appearance. But he was fun, educated, and could hold his own with her. Still Abby pushed the thought from her mind.

"Oh, Mark, could you grab my *Vanity Fair* out of the bag?"

Mark sighed and jumped up, pulling the bag back to the floor.

"It's in the front pocket," she kind of purred.

He pulled the magazine out, handed it to Abby, and once again lifted the bag to the bin. Mission accomplished, he plopped down onto his seat.

"You're the man, Marky Mark. Thanks," she said with a warm smile, and opened her magazine.

"That's me." Mark pulled his cell from his pocket and checked his email.

Abby glanced at Mark and asked, "Anything interesting? Is the company still standing in our absence?"

Mark smiled and replied, "Yes, and I have the emails to prove it." He shoved the phone back into his pocket and said, "The toughest part of being gone is missing out on the betting in my group's fantasy football league."

Abby laid the magazine on her lap. "You actually play and bet on that with your people?"

"Yeah. I consider it departmental team-building."

"Aren't you afraid that you'll be viewed as just one of the guys?" she asked. "And not the leader? Doesn't it get distracting and ridiculously time consuming?"

Mark shrugged. "Naw. It doesn't change how they view me."

"What about you?" Mark asked, shifting in his seat. "What are you doing in the name of team-building?"

"I wouldn't call that team-building. Anyway, my group doesn't need much direction and personal interaction. Sales are a tough part of Collier's business, so I don't have much time for male bonding sessions." She laughed.

Mark smiled. "But what are you doing to connect with them? To build your group? To have fun?"

"What do you suggest?" Abby asked. "Setting up a Wii in the office?"

"No. But how will you get to know your people, to connect with them?" He teasingly added, "And in turn create your successor so you and I can sail off to a private island?"

Abby laughed. "I've got it covered and I don't like rum by the way." She lifted her magazine, ending the conversation. But as she scanned the fashion-filled photos, Abby realized that Mark was getting to her in more ways than one.

■   ■   ■

LARRY WESLEY followed his wife, Tina, onto the plane. Before they took their customary seats in first class, Larry stood in the galley that separated the two cabins and comically waved and peered at his team members sitting in coach. He was greeted with a few cheers and whistles.

Larry walked up front, sat down and connected his seatbelt.

"We've been on the plane for 30 seconds, and everyone back there already knows you," Tina commented.

"It's always important to meet your fellow travelers, because they could be the last people you see," he joked.

"Not funny," she replied nervously. Tina had never enjoyed flying and only did so when the allure of the destination could overpower her anxiety. A luxurious ski lodge and spa had qualified. Still, she would maintain an iron grip on Larry's hand during takeoff.

A flight attendant approached and asked, "Good morning. We have a few minutes before our departure, so would you like something to drink?"

"Definitely," Tina replied. "A vodka cranberry. That should help."

The attendant smiled and turned to Larry. "And you, sir?"

Larry had no interest in liquor at 9:00 a.m. He ordered a coffee.

The attendant left and Larry commented, "I know there's no point in telling you to relax but...relax."

"Right." Tina leaned back into her seat. "I'll relax in about two hours."

Larry slid his briefcase from under his seat and withdrew the report that had kept Penny awake all night. He noted the timestamp from when the report was generated. Midnight. Making progress.

Larry began to flip at random through the report but his mind was elsewhere. Even though his team was making their usual trip at the usual time of the year, Larry recognized that this retreat would be different.

The primary reason, he believed, were the 360s, from which all manner of team discussion had flowed. People were continuing to do their jobs and working as a group, but attitudes had perceptibly shifted a bit since the reports were presented. He was seeing a curiosity about the process and everyone was getting more comfortable with their feedback. There was less resentment and more openness.

Larry understood that the 360 itself hadn't caused the problems. They had already existed. The report just pulled back the curtain to expose the team's professional issues. Yet Larry at times still struggled to understand just how this level of knowledge and self-realization was going to help anyone. Sometimes, he mused, ignorance is indeed bliss.

In his case he would have preferred to have never seen the report. Larry's ego had suffered a direct hit. Did these people really want their leader to be overly accommodating? For him to waste effort on being a "corporate cheerleader" instead of simply being a strong and forceful leader? For him to waste time casting unrealistically optimistic visions of the future? To force a greeting with the building's security guard each morning?

The attendant returned with their drinks and Larry absently poured sugar into his mug. As he stirred the coffee, Larry acknowledged the other difference on this trip.

▓   ▓   ▓

PAIGE smiled and made her way back to the coach cabin. Paige greeted each team member before settling in. She retrieved a new business book by Patrick Lencioni and a bottle of water from her bag and placed the case in the overhead compartment. She slid into her seat and looked out the window. It was a beautiful, clear day without a single cloud blemishing the deep blue sky. They would have a great view all the way to Utah. Paige watched through the window as the plane slowly retreated from the gate.

Paige leaned back into her seat and considered not just their destination, but how they had arrived here. Collier's journey through the assessment was not unique or even unusual. No one—no matter how self aware or eager to make personal improvements—enjoys hearing critiques from bosses, peers or direct reports. The strongest leaders usually have the strongest wills and deepest wells of confidence. Yet nothing scales those formidable walls faster than honest feedback.

With today's speed to market, those leading the team could no longer afford to overlook their areas of development. There was a new business climate in the wind, driven by a global explosion of innovative, competitive companies that weren't limited by geography. No longer could companies simply keep up with the guy next door. They now had to watch out for the guy on the next continent.

Paige sipped her water and watched as the plane began rolling down a runway. Collier was indeed at the forefront of solar technologies and an industry that was set to transform how people received and used energy. Even Sun Chips was using solar power in their food manufacturing plants. But, before Collier could change with their solar panels, they would first need to make some genuine changes in themselves.

The plane gathered speed and shot down the runway, lifting from the ground into the sky above. Yes, Collier needed to make changes, Paige thought, as the ground quickly shrank beneath them. She was pretty sure that she could help them get there.

Chapter 11

Laurel Peak Resort

LAUREL PEAK Resort was a five-star resort located near Sundance, Utah. The resort featured amenities such as a hot-springs spa, a variety of outdoor activities, and beautiful meeting and conference rooms with wood burning fireplaces for corporate getaways. It was here that Collier's leadership retreat would take place.

The resort was also unique in one way: It had recently become one of the first ski resorts to install solar panels to generate energy. During the summer months, the panels would provide more than half of the resort's energy needs as the ski trails turned into mountain bike paths.

Part of Collier's corporate mandate was to do business with companies with whom they maintained business relationships. The annual leadership retreat always took place at a property that was actively using or planning to utilize a Collier solar product.

These company retreats allowed Collier to accomplish complementary goals. They could see firsthand the results of their new energy products and technology. And because Abby, her team, and Larry were the contacts for Collier's customers, the retreats allowed every senior team member to meet their customers, solidifying the client relationship.

Every aspect of the retreat was planned in detailed precision. Group sessions, workshops, and a client roundtable, all balanced with precious downtime. Yet even the best plans were subject to the unexpected.

■   ■   ■

PAIGE stood with her arms folded and surveyed the rustic, comfortable, conference room. Local plants and flowers were displayed at each corner of the room. A side table was filled with seasonal fruits, juices, polished carafes of coffee, and crystal pitchers of water. Another table held fresh muffins, buttery croissants, and platters of fresh bagels and imported cheeses and butters.

The conference table was dotted with binders for each chair. At the far end of the room, a stone hearth provided a crackling fire. Hopefully, Paige mused, no one would be lured to sleep by the warm surroundings. While the surroundings were beautiful, the emphasis was still on getting the team to work together.

While each leader was growing more comfortable with Paige—and receptive to addressing personal issues—she knew that it was a process, not an event with incorporating the feedback. And she wasn't looking for perfection, just progress. Paige also realized it was somewhat awkward to discuss the 360 in a group setting. Everyone at the table understood that their critical comments had been written by the very people around them.

Still, Paige was confident that she was making pretty good progress with each leader. Larry, as expected, was more challenging than the rest. As with most strong leaders, he maintained a style that did not respond well to feedback. Paige realized that her biggest challenge was to convince Larry of how feedback could benefit him personally. This challenge was probably the most vital. If Larry could become a little more open and honest, and publicly commit to goals for his growth and development, the team would follow suit. How exactly to move Larry forward, however, was the issue.

※　※　※

SHORTLY before 1:00 that afternoon, Collier's leadership team began trickling into the conference room. Paige took a quick read of each member as they arrived. Everyone seemed in high spirits. Paige knew that new environments could inject energy into meetings and conversations that may feel mundane at the home office.

After everyone had eaten, Larry stood at the head of the table and addressed the group.

"Welcome, everyone, to Collier's annual leadership retreat. I'm your host, Larry Wesley."

The leaders clapped and whistled.

"As you've seen, Laurel Peak is a fantastic resort. It's a leader in resort companies that are taking the initiative in implementing new energy in their operations. I've also saved a special announcement for this morning. Laurel Peak was recently awarded the Green Power Leadership Award from the EPA in recognition of their Collier-produced seventh generation solar panels."

Everyone again cheered.

"The press release is going out next week. This is a tremendous honor for Laurel Peak and, just as importantly, for Collier Energy. This award is a culmination of the hard work and effort put forth by all of you. Each of you is integral to what we do, and each of you is essential to my team. And while this award is a great honor, Collier is just getting started."

The leaders clapped.

"We have a lot of ground to cover over the next few days," Larry said. "But we've also included some free time to relax. Your itineraries are included in the binders." Larry indicated the folders on the table.

"First on our agenda is a 360 workshop, facilitated by Paige Darnell.

"I want to thank Paige for making this trip with us and contributing to our retreat. She has become an important part of Collier's leadership development strategy. And with that, Paige..." he said, gesturing to her. Larry took a seat, and Paige took his place at the head of the table.

"Thank you, Larry," Paige replied. "And congratulations to all of you on winning this amazing award. It's a remarkable tribute to your talent and hard work."

Paige looked around the table. "I want to open by saying what a privilege it has been to partner with your team. You are an intelligent, hardworking, and dedicated group of leaders."

Paige paused and then continued, "I know the 360 assessment is not the easiest thing to experience. I know that it's challenging to receive feedback from your colleagues.

"But I also know that feedback through a 360-Degree Report can significantly enhance a leadership team more than any other approach. It's boot camp, it's getting down to the real stuff. I've done these assessments for over 20 years, and in that time I have seen the 360 assessment change lives.

"I recommend you not only solicit feedback from your colleagues for the rest of your professional careers but from your clients as well. It is the best way to stay at the top of your business.

"You began this journey with the direction to honestly evaluate your peers. This takes tremendous courage, because none of you has any desire to harm someone else on the team. Yet I'm willing to bet that you did the assessments because you wanted to help your fellow leaders grow and get past any blind spots.

"You've each done the assessments. And you've each received a report. You've had time to consider your feedback. So let's talk about how this information can positively impact your role and growth at Collier."

■   ■   ■

PAIGE directed each person in the group to open their binders.

"Let me start by telling you the goals of this workshop. First, this session will help you understand others' perceptions of you as a leader. Every person around us has a unique and different perspective than our own. Each can offer insights we would otherwise miss.

"Second, you'll identify your top strengths and ways in which you can leverage them. We're often told to focus all of our effort on improving our weaknesses. But, in reality, we are best served by developing our strengths into excellence. And improving our weaknesses to a level where they don't hurt our performance. As senior leaders, you do need a general understanding in every key area at Collier. While you don't have to be exceptional at everything, you do have to be exceptional in using your strengths in your various roles.

"Third, you'll prioritize and address your areas of opportunity. This is a key part of the process.

"Fourth, you'll create a short, crisp action plan with no more than 3 areas of development for your leadership growth. This is the part of the assessment process where words become actions. As you know from your business, the best plans and ideas are meaningless without clear strategic implementation.

"And fifth, you'll learn an effective follow-up process, ways in which you can gauge, measure and evaluate your growth and development and stay accountable to it.

"I know I sound like I'm stuck on repeat, but this bears mentioning one more time. Last time." Paige smiled. "In all of the companies I've worked with, and in all of the years I've spent being a facilitator, I have to yet to see a team not benefit positively from conducting feedback assessments. In every type of organization, it will enhance the workplace, the leadership team, and your success as a company.

"So, on that note, let's talk about the reports."

■   ■   ■

"LET'S start with a question," Paige said. "At what temperature does water boil?"

After a moment of silence, Melissa offered, "212 degrees."

Paige nodded. "That's right. Not 210 or even 211. You must have that extra degree to make it boil.

"In a steam engine, 211 degrees is ineffective at creating energy. But by adding just one more degree, you can produce dramatically different results.

"The point?" Paige asked. "One degree can make a tremendous difference. Just a little more effort in the right areas will bring significant change. A tipping point. The difference between 211 and 212 on paper is miniscule and looks irrelevant. But, in the real world, one degree is huge.

"In our professional performance," Paige said. "If we put in that extra effort, heat things up a little more, we can create different results.

"That's what the strength section of the assessment is all about. You're already good in many, but not all, of the seven areas. The 360 offers you the chance to see these positives on paper. You can then leverage that strength in the real world through actions, adding that one extra degree, to really build on where you excel."

Paige surveyed the table. "Feedback is what the 360 is all about. So the next part of the workshop will build on the benefit of different perspectives."

Paige held up a sample report. "Let's turn to the final page of the report," Paige said. "You'll recognize the Top 10 list, competencies where you're the strongest. What I'd like you to do is to break up into groups of two and discuss your top three strengths, taking advantage of a perspective different than your own.

"And," Paige continued, "if you feel comfortable doing so, I would recommend that you also discuss three from the Bottom 10 as well. I understand if you feel uncomfortable doing that. But I promise you, it's ultimately worth it.

"Remember," Paige advised, "discussing opportunities for growth can impact and enhance what you do. None of us is perfect, and each of us has areas in which we could pursue growth. So this isn't about criticism. It's about helping each other find ways to grow in our roles and, as a result, enhance the entire team. So no one—not here, not anywhere—is beyond finding ways to grow.

"Around the lobby's perimeter are small rooms that I've reserved for each group. The pairs are Abby and Mark, Doug and Penny, and Jim and Melissa. Your names are affixed to the plates by each door. Larry," she nodded in his direction, "You and I can meet here.

"Please take your reports with you. And if you feel comfortable, consider sharing additional information from your results, beyond the Top 10 and Bottom 10."

Paige glanced at the wall clock. "I've scheduled one hour for these meetings, so each person has 30 minutes to discuss their report. But I've also scheduled a half-hour break after that hour, in case your session runs long. So let's meet back here at 4:00."

Everyone stood and began collecting their bags and binders. Paige watched the leaders exit the room and considered the next part of the workshop. Over the past few weeks, as she had met with and observed each leader, Paige had also analyzed each person's report and compared them with the other leaders' assessments. She had then partnered each person with someone whose strengths counterbalanced the other's weaknesses, and vice-versa. Paige hoped that these strategic partnerships would allow leaders to receive valuable, and qualified, insight from each other.

"So, Paige," Larry said, interrupting her thoughts. "To what do I owe the privilege of this one-on-one meeting?"

"Odd numbers?"

Larry smiled. "Do I have time to quickly run to my room?"

Chapter 12

The Strengths and Challenges of Mark

ABBY and Mark sat in a small lounge on the resort's main floor. The room contained soft, comfortable furnishings, a coffee table, and a stone fireplace. Abby sat on a love seat, while Mark leaned back in a recliner. They stared at the hypnotic flames, each lost in their own thoughts, delaying a potentially awkward conversation.

Mark took in the surroundings and finally remarked, "This room doesn't seem very conducive to working."

"I think this room is more conducive to conversation," Abby replied. "Warm, pleasant. Glowing fire. It's about making us comfortable."

"Any more comfortable and I may fall asleep," Mark said.

"Well, let's get uncomfortable then." Abby chuckled. "Let's get out your report."

Mark sighed. "I've got the report right here," he said, tapping his forehead. "Unfortunately. What would you like to know?"

"Well, let's start with the positives. Because I know your pluses have to outweigh any perceived negatives."

Mark slightly smiled. "Let's see," he said, shifting in his chair, collecting his thoughts. "I'm, apparently, very knowledgeable."

"Absolutely."

"I'm considered very trustworthy."

"Certainly."

"And I'm good at building my team."

"Definitely. Great. Your portion of the meeting is adjourned."

Mark laughed.

"So?" Abby asked. "Thoughts on that feedback?"

Mark pulled a knee up with both hands. "Well, honestly, I'm not entirely surprised. I like to believe I'm good in those areas."

Abby nodded.

Mark thought a moment and then said, "I think I'm kind of an IT anomaly. Or, at least, an anomaly to the IT stereotype. You know, all about computers and systems, not very good at people skills. I really enjoy working and interacting with people. I could never be content just sitting in front of multiple monitors, only solving the world's technology problems."

Abby again nodded.

"I like my team, and part of that is a desire to see them grow and develop at Collier, in the industry, or wherever their careers take them. So, I'm pleased to hear that my team see that."

"Of course we do."

Mark stared at the fire and said, "But apparently there's a flip side to my interest in connecting with people."

"How so?"

Mark thought a moment, and then chose to go for broke, for complete honesty. Besides, he thought, Abby was one of Larry's confidants, anyway.

"Larry shared a concern with me a few weeks ago," Mark began slowly. "He feels that I'm often overly friendly with clients and team members. So much so that I move into conversation or correspondence that can come off as too casual, or even inappropriate. His words, not mine."

Abby nodded.

"But it's harmless," Mark insisted. "I don't like being stuffy with people inside or outside the office. Why shouldn't our jobs be fun? So, if I send an edgy YouTube video, or a forward with a joke, what's the harm?"

Abby considered the question and said, "Mark, it's great that you enjoy people, and try to connect with them."

"But."

She smiled. "There are a few buts. First, most of us get too many emails already, and we don't have time to open silly YouTubes. I just delete forwards without ever reading them. They have been mostly annoying time wasters. So send YouTube forwards very selectively. Otherwise, you look like a goof-off."

Mark sighed. "Next."

"Next, you never know where an email will end up. As a rule, if you would feel uncomfortable with anyone besides the intended receiver seeing the contents of that email, don't write it. Better yet, err on being overcautious by keeping every email professional."

Mark didn't reply.

"And finally, when you send an email, your address includes Collier's name. Every time, you're representing the company, in-house or to the outside world. So when you hit send, always consider whether your email best represents Collier."

Mark exhaled deeply. "Okay, I will begrudgingly concede that you make some valid points. But I still think it's overkill to keep everything so stiff and formal."

"I won't presume to speak for Larry, but I don't think he's going that far. Conversationally, it's natural to be a bit casual. You don't want to come off as a robot. But the written word can so easily be misconstrued. There's no body language, no facial expressions, to convey the tone of a message. It's best to just play it safe."

Mark grunted a reply.

They stared at the fire for a few moments, each lost in their thoughts. Finally Abby said lightly, "Well, this is not how I pictured a fireside evening in a fabulous ski resort."

Mark stirred. "Oh, yeah?"

"No. I was thinking of…" She hesitated and said, "Well, not a coworker."

"That would be wise, I guess," Mark conceded. He was now genuinely curious and asked, "What are some requirements for a fireside kind of guy in a 5 star resort?"

Abby laughed. "Let's see," she said, sitting up. "A man that comes from old money would be nice. New money would be fine, too. Tiffany & Co. takes both, I believe."

Mark laughed. "What's good enough for Tiffany should be good enough for you."

"Right. Next, I would really prefer an Ivy League man."

"No problem," Mark remarked dryly. "Those guys are a dime-a-dozen."

"Finally," she said, "He needs to have impeccable style."

"Like what?" Mark asked. "Italian-made, tailored suits?"

"Oh, yes. Please." She laughed.

"Why are his clothes so important?" Mark asked. "I mean, not to get all psychological on you, but shouldn't who he is matter as much as what he wears?"

"Of course. That's number four on the list. Character."

Mark smirked. "Uh-huh."

"Listen," Abby said, "in defense of my alleged shallowness, a guy in well-tailored clothes tells me something important before we even meet."

"Such as?"

"That he's likely successful, or on track to become successful, or at least pursuing success. That he cares about his appearance and his impression on others. That he wants to be taken seriously. Trust me, when it comes to women, grooming is a big deal."

"I'll take your word for it, I guess."

"How people dress is important for all kinds of reasons," Abby said. "It helps people form an immediate impression of us. It may not be fair, or even right, but it tells people a lot about us before we even speak." Abby laughed. "Wow, I could write a book on this."

Mark chuckled. "All of that makes sense in your world, Abby. First impressions are very critical to what you do. I understand the value of impressions when it comes to sales. But not everyone needs to dress like they're closing the big deal right after lunch at The Four Seasons."

"You don't think impressions are important at the office, too?" she asked.

"No." Mark shifted in his chair. "I mean, not entirely." He paused a moment then said, "I don't know. I didn't think so."

"Until now?" Abby joked. "I've helped you see the light? I *am* a fashion messiah!"

Mark smiled weakly and replied, "No, the doubt started creeping in after I received my group feedback."

Abby slightly nodded, knowing that she too had mentioned Mark's appearance on his 360.

"Can you handle a moment of true confession?" Mark asked.

Mark stared at the fire and said, "I know I'm not the best dresser at the office. But, honestly, it's never been a concern of mine. Are my clothes in style? Probably not. Are they tailored? Definitely not. But here's the thing: I was hired for my skill set. And, if you'll indulge me in a self-congratulatory moment, we have a network system that runs very smoothly."

Abby held up her cell with a smirk.

Mark smiled. "Generally smoothly. But seriously, I was hired because of my expertise. I moved into this position because of what I can do, not how I look while doing it. That standard, in my position, doesn't seem applicable or right."

"I get that," Abby said, measuring her reply. "But Mark, it's not just the front line people, such as my team, who form public impressions of Collier. As we continue to grow, we'll begin to hold more and more in-house client meetings. Meetings that you'll need to attend. And appearance, I would argue, is a big part of shaping the client perception of our company."

Mark didn't reply.

"Plus, I would even go so far as to say that our personal image instills confidence in our clients," Abby said.

Mark again didn't reply.

"Look, Mark," Abby said, "I understand where you're coming from. I realize that some people don't have a natural inclination toward clothing and grooming. You probably have zero interest in going to buy clothes, right?"

Mark smiled. "I loathe shopping for clothes."

"Okay, and then on the other end of the spectrum, you have someone like me who lives to shop for clothes. To shop for anything, actually. But it just so happens that my personal interest in fashion benefits me in my job as well.

"So, yes," Abby continued, "this comes easy to me. And yes," she smiled, "that fact may make this advice sound annoying coming from me. But the truth remains. What this means for you is that you'll have to step out of your comfort zone to address this issue."

Mark stared up at the ceiling and exhaled deeply. "It's not just about clothing. Apparently my appearance is also lacking in my office. As in the physical space."

He thought a moment then said, "I know that my office looks a little..."

"...like a disaster zone?" Abby teased.

Mark smiled. "I was searching for something else. Like colorfully funky and intriguingly unkempt. And my filing probably seems... unorthodox."

"You certainly have your own innovative system," Abby remarked. "It's beyond me how you find anything."

"But, see, I do find things," Mark said. "And I get work done. A lot of work. And everything in my department runs very well. So I don't understand how my office, my own personal area, is a problem for anyone else. I'm the one who has to work there. And, if I'm getting the work done and doing the job well, why do I need to change?"

Abby considered her next words. "Mark, I don't think the 360 is critiquing your job performance," she said carefully. "You're extremely dedicated to your role, to Larry, and to your team. But again, fair or not, appearance matters. Especially in business."

"Let me ask you this," Abby said. "If you walked into Larry's office and he had files stacked all over the floor, how would you view that?"

Mark was silent and then said, "Okay, I admit, that would bother me."

"I'm betting that environment wouldn't inspire confidence in Larry as a leader."

Mark didn't reply.

"Larry is a great leader, of course. So a messy office wouldn't accurately reflect his leadership ability. But the appearance still matters. Because while the appearance wouldn't define him, it would harm people's impressions of him."

Mark sighed. "Right."

"Here's one more perspective for you. If someone entered your office without knowing who you are and what your job is, and without knowing your title, what do you think their impression would be?"

Mark threw up his hands in mock frustration. "Okay, okay! I give."

Abby thought a moment and said, "You know, if you wanted help finding clothes, I would be happy to help you."

Mark cocked an eyebrow. "Really?"

"Sure," Abby said. "I've secretly always wanted to be your personal shopper. And I shouldn't hoard my fashion genius. I need to share it with the less fortunate."

Mark laughed. "You're too kind."

Abby smiled. "But I'm serious. I would love to help."

"So," Mark said lightly, "are you asking me on some kind of shopping date?"

Abby felt her face flush. "Hum. Maybe."

"I don't know," he teased. "Me. You. Your favorite pastime."

"Alright, don't flatter yourself," Abby replied regaining her composure. "I'm just doing my part to improve Collier's image."

Mark smiled. "Okay."

Abby couldn't believe she actually felt nervous. She switched topics and said, "So, Dr. Phil. Now it's my turn on the couch. Luckily, I'm already on one."

Chapter 13

Abby Receives Unvarnished Counsel

ABBY pulled her computer bag from the floor. She unzipped the front of the bag and retrieved her 360 report from the pocket. Abby began to open the report and then hesitated.

"Consider yourself privileged, Mark," Abby said. "I'm not really the sharing type."

"It's an honor," Mark replied sincerely.

Abby laughed. "And I certainly never confess to anything less than perfection, professionally or otherwise."

"You're not perfect?"

"Well, I am *almost* perfect. So very close. I'm a neighbor to perfect." She tapped the report with a manicured fingernail. "And I even have proof."

"Please share."

"Okay," Abby said, opening the report. "Let's treat this as we would an employee review, shall we? Sugar first, then the medicine."

"I'm sure we're dealing with 95% sugar, anyway."

"Right. So, let's see," Abby said, flipping through the report. "First up, Knowledge. No problem there."

"It does help to know what one is selling."

"I do try," Abby said. "Innovation? Score. Character? Pretty Solid. Execution? Done, like, yesterday."

"Sounds good," Mark replied. "Meeting adjourned?"

"And then," Abby continued, "We have Professionalism. I..." Abby paused, softening her praise. "I, uh, did pretty well here."

"It's fine, Abby," Mark said, dismissively waving his hand. "I'm a big boy. I can handle it. Besides, you were born wearing Armani booties. You deserve your accolades."

Abby thought a moment and then said, "I know that, and I get it. Yet..." Abby trailed off. After a moment she said, "Yet this feedback is tough to take. Especially since I'm primarily receiving it from my very own team. People I always look out for. Fight for. Protect."

Mark nodded.

"My team is fantastic," Abby said. "We are absolutely rocking in sales right now. At this rate, I may be able to retire at 40."

Mark laughed.

Abby looked into the fire. "But this same team, this very successful team, is telling me that I'm self-centered and don't really care about developing them unless it helps me."

"Really?"

"Well, not exactly," Abby said, perplexed. "I was rated highly in Leadership. Great feedback, in fact. That's what makes these negative comments so confusing."

Mark nodded.

"It's like a feedback paradox," Abby said. "I'm a great leader, but apparently everyone feels I'm lousy at *creating* leaders. Or in 360 terminology, Building Talent."

Mark again nodded.

"It's hard for me to understand this perspective," Abby continued. "Sales is a tough world. You have to develop thick skin to do well. My team is tenacious and aggressive in making the sales, yet for some reason, they want me to hold their hands and coddle them."

"How so?" Mark asked.

"Look, I came up in sales the old-fashioned way. Through hard work, persistence, and an unwillingness to ever take no for an answer. I have strived, I have pursued, and I have persevered. No one handed me this job. No one hands you anything in the business world. You have to get it yourself."

"Okay," Mark said.

"And, if I may indulge in a potentially sexist complaint, I have obtained all of this as a woman. I mean, I'm not going to sit here and whine and say, 'Woe is me.' But let's be honest, while there may be a few advantages to being a woman in business, the disadvantages are there as well."

Mark didn't reply.

"I got here and achieved my success through hard work and talent. So I don't understand the need for grooming anyone. In the sales world, leaders are groomed through natural selection. Survival of the fittest. Do a good job, work hard, learn everything you can about the business, and success is a natural result."

Mark cleared his throat and said, "I understand what you're saying. And there's no doubt that success results from hard work. But I think, in this instance, Building Talent is not about babying your team, or helping them into easy, undeserved promotions."

"Then what is it?"

"It's about imparting your knowledge to others. Sharing wisdom that can help them grow. Pouring yourself into those whom you feel could benefit from your insights."

"How?" Abby asked in an exasperated tone. "By playing online sporting games with them?"

"No," Mark said slowly. "That doesn't really fall under this category. Granted, I do interact with my team in ways that may blur the leader/direct report relationship. I get that. But you know what? I can tell you what is going on in their lives. Who's dating someone seriously. Who's going through a breakup. Whose kids are playing what sports."

"What on earth does that have to do with building talent, may I ask?"

"Nothing directly," Mark replied. "But by attempting to connect with them, and by taking an interest in them outside of their roles, I'm able to better know them. To better understand them." Mark shifted in his seat to look at Abby. "This is all an aside really. I'm not suggesting that you hang out with your direct reports outside the office like I do. That's not the point."

"So what is the point?"

"The point," Mark said, "is that building talent involves taking an active interest in your team members. It doesn't have to look like what I do. And the online sports thing has nothing to do with this. But it is an example of how I connect with my group."

Abby didn't reply.

"Let's move on from the personal bonding aspect," Mark said. "Because, again, that's not the point.

"Look at it another way," Mark suggested. "Let's change the semantics. Let's move from building talent to mentoring. I know you've worked hard to get where you are. It's no accident that you lead the sales team. But certainly along the way, you've had people mentor you."

Abby thought a moment and then said, "Sort of. But my career is still the result of my hard work."

"If I recall," Mark said, "Larry was an advocate for your promotion into this position after the last guy left."

Abby started to respond but Mark held up his hands and said, "Wait. Just give me a minute here. I'm not saying you didn't deserve to be promoted. Again, we've already established that you've worked very hard to get where you are.

"But, at the same time," Mark continued, "Larry took an active interest in your professional growth and development. He was a key advocate for your taking on that role. Would that be fair to say?"

"Sure," Abby replied. "Larry has always been very supportive."

"And would it be fair to say that Larry helped you grow professionally?"

Abby was silent.

Mark said, "See, Larry's support doesn't detract from the fact that you're talented, or from the reality that you've worked hard. Larry's support and your hard work aren't mutually exclusive. They're complementary."

Abby didn't respond.

"So my question is this," Mark said quietly. "Do you think Larry's input and private and public support helped you move to the next stage of your career?"

Abby exhaled deeply and said, "Okay. Yes."

"Look Abby, you're one of the most candid people I know. So give me some latitude, just for now, to be just as candid with you."

Abby nodded hesitantly.

"You don't seem interested in giving back to others what Larry has provided to you."

Abby started and said, "Wow, Mark. You said candid, not brutal."

"Hey, this isn't any fun for me," Mark said. "And what do I have to gain by being this honest? I'm only telling you this because I think you are amazingly gifted and have a lot to share with your team."

Abby stared at the fire and smiled slightly.

"You know, building talent actually benefits you, too."

"Finally," Abby joked weakly. "A silver lining to my 360 cloud."

Mark smiled. "Investing in your people will positively impact your team, and you, in a few ways.

"For one thing, morale would be improved. People will respond positively only if they feel you're taking an interest in helping them learn and grow. No one ever complains that the boss is too interested in helping them succeed."

"Noted," Abby said. "Next."

"Next, taking an interest in them allows you to better develop their skills and talents. Which, again, benefits you too, as your team becomes more effective in making sales."

"I think I read that somewhere."

"Right. Part of taking an interest in them is sharing your knowledge and wisdom with your team. This will really contribute to their growth." Mark teased, "Why hoard all of your amazing wisdom and genius for yourself?"

"That *would* be selfish."

"Really, this is all about grooming the next group of leaders. Sure, we invest in our people so they can become more effective in their jobs. But what we should be doing is identifying those with leadership potential and then grooming them for those roles." He paused and said, "For our roles, actually."

"Great, now I'm training my replacement," Abby smirked.

"In a way, yeah," Mark said. "Do you see yourself being the VP of Sales for the next ten years?"

Abby considered the question and replied, "No." She paused again and said, "I eventually want to do bigger and better things."

"Well, then, someone will need to take your place. Why not start preparing the most talented individuals for that transition now?"

Abby cracked a slight smile. "Mark, I will admit, I'm impressed with your insights on this."

"Really?" Mark asked, doubtful.

"Really."

"Thanks for the compliment."

"I get what you're saying, but I'm not entirely sure what all of this looks like for my team. I still think the cream rises to the top, with or without input from a superior."

"Maybe so. But try to remember how Larry has impacted your career at Collier, how he has invested in you as a person and a leader."

"I see that," Abby said. "But Larry and I have a natural rapport. That doesn't just happen with just any person. While I value each of my team members, I don't necessarily have that kind of relationship with everyone."

"Okay," Mark replied. "But at least you can think about it."

"I wouldn't worry about that," Abby replied, gathering her things. "I've definitely been thinking about all of this since I received my assessment."

Mark pulled the recliner upright and slid on his shoes. "Yeah, I can relate."

"So did we accomplish our mission for this meeting?" Abby asked, rising from the love seat.

Mark also stood and replied, "I think so." He thought a moment and said, "I think you helped me see a different take on my issue."

"And you too," Abby said.

"And hopefully," Mark added, "my honesty won't affect my chances of a shopping date. Or our life on that island paradise."

Abby laughed. "Let's start with the working wardrobe first. Island boy will have to wait."

"Let's do both, then."

Abby looked at Mark and cracked a smile. "Okay." Abby slid her bag's strap over her shoulder. "So what now?" she asked, again shifting the subject. "We have a half hour until we reconvene with Paige.

Chapter 14

Doug Struggles

DOUG and Penny entered the small lounge and took in their surroundings. The room faced the main slope, and a large window offered a view of skiers making their way down the brilliant white mountainside. Two armchairs faced the window, and Doug and Penny each took a seat.

Doug let his computer bag slip to the floor and commented, "What a view."

Penny nodded and replied, "Yes. This is how I prefer to experience a ski course. Vicariously."

"What, no desire to showcase your skill on the slopes?"

Penny smiled. "Oh, no. I consider myself athletically *dis*inclined."

"I'm sure you'd be fine," Doug said, his gaze following the chairlift up the hill. "I'm going to give it a go this weekend. It's been a while, though, so come back here with your video camera to capture the highlights of my downhill."

Penny laughed.

Both sat in silence for a moment, enjoying the sights and muffled sounds of people at play, each wanting to delay the topic at hand.

Doug finally spoke up and said lightly, "Well, shall we get started?"

Penny nodded and said, "I guess so. Are you volunteering to go first?"

"I guess so," he replied. Doug unzipped his bag and retrieved the 360 report. He turned to Penny and said, "I've got to say, I'm glad this is you in here. It makes it a little easier to talk about my report."

"I appreciate that, Doug. I'm glad you can trust me."

Doug grimaced slightly and opened his report.

"Well," Doug said, "Paige said to begin with the positives, so let's see." He scanned through a few pages and then said, "Okay... Leadership. I did well there, although admittedly, my direct reports total two people."

Penny smiled and said, "Still, you're a great leader in a very important role. You don't just lead people; you spearhead employee programs, shape our benefit packages, and recruit the very best talent. Doug, I'd say you do a tremendous job."

Doug returned her smile. "Thanks, Penny." He turned back to the report and flipped a few pages. "Innovation? Good, but again, my role doesn't require much of that." He turned a few more pages and said, "Professionalism, pretty good, too. Really, I did well overall."

"That's not surprising," Penny remarked.

"Except..." Doug trailed off and watched through the window as someone careened wildly down the slope and then wiped out. He pointed through the glass at the wayward skier. "See that? That is probably me tomorrow."

Penny laughed.

Doug chuckled and then returned to his previous thought. He considered his next words and then nodded to himself and said, "I'm pleased with almost every aspect of my report. Except for one area."

"Okay," Penny said, nodding encouragingly.

"One glaring area that is pretty much consuming my thoughts both inside and outside the office."

Doug sighed and said, "Apparently, people at the office consider me untrustworthy. Peers, even my direct reports, all seem to be in agreement that I am not to be completely trusted with information."

"Surely the comments aren't that strongly worded," Penny said.

"Well, no," Doug conceded. "Not exactly. The actual words aren't necessarily harsh. But the implications, the underlying meanings, what I read between the lines—all terrible. Strong language isn't needed. Because when someone talks about your being trustworthy, they're really talking about your character. And if your character is bad, aren't you pretty much beyond redemption?"

"Now, Doug," Penny said, "I can't believe that people are actually attacking your character here. If you feel comfortable, why don't you share a couple of the comments with me so we can discuss it?"

Doug nodded and picked up his report. He turned to the Trustworthiness section, selected a comment and said, "Okay. Here's one. 'While Doug's personality and role naturally encourages others to talk with him, he has a tendency to share confidential information of a personal nature with other people.'"

Penny's face remained impassive as she listened intently to her own comment being read back to her.

"See?" Doug said. "Character flaw."

"Let's hear another comment," Penny said.

Doug frowned and turned back to the report. "'While Doug is a great listener, he unfortunately is an even bigger talker. He has at times shared with me private information about other employees, which leads me to assume I have likewise been discussed.' Ouch."

"Okay," Penny said, "Just one more."

Doug glanced at Penny. "Are we feeling sadistic?"

"No, I think I may have a point."

Doug looked uncertain but turned again to the report. "Doug seems to indulge in office gossip that could be harmful to other people.'" He closed the binder and tossed it aside. "So, how can anything in that section contribute to my growth? The damage is done, my reputation tarnished. How can I even look people in the eye anymore, knowing what they think of me?"

"Doug, I don't believe this is about character. Yes, it does fall under Trustworthiness on the report. But I don't think anyone believes you have poor character."

"How can you interpret this any other way?" Doug asked in frustration. "Trustworthiness and character are practically synonymous."

Penny thought a moment and said, "First, these comments are addressing a behavior, not a trait. And behaviors can be modified. Right?"

"Sure," Doug said. "But my behavior, or people's interpretation of my behavior, I should say, indicates that they feel I have bad character."

"I don't agree," Penny said. "Let me tell you why. What's happening here is that one of your strengths is being overused and possibly having a negative impact."

"How's that?"

"Okay," Penny began, "just for the sake of argument, let's interpret these comments literally. No reading between the lines. You shared information that was confided in you. Period."

"Okay," Doug said warily.

"But why did someone share with you in the first place?" Penny asked.

Doug thought a moment and said, "I don't know. Tell me."

"Because you're such a great person to talk to," Penny observed. "You're a great listener. You take an active interest in other people, and it's apparent. People are going to be drawn to someone like that."

Doug didn't reply.

"And why are you a great listener? Because you love to connect with people. It's a part of your job, of course. But it's a very natural part of who you are."

Doug considered this.

"Just think of your job title—Human Resources. That says it all, right? And it's what you excel in. You thrive on working with people, communicating with people."

Doug slowly nodded. "Okay. But how does this tie in to my concerns?"

"Doug, you love to connect with people. But it's possible…" she hesitated then decided to be honest. "No, *I* believe that your desire to connect takes a negative turn at times."

Doug recognized Penny's shift from impersonal to personal observations. Yet, he trusted Penny and knew that she would never intentionally try to harm him.

"Part of connecting with others is sharing," Penny said. "It's not about one-way communication, right? It's back and forth. So what happens is you tend to share with others, but you share the wrong things.

"Let's just be honest," Penny said. "Sharing secrets is a bonding experience. And a hint of conspiracy is exciting to people. So, again, I think all of this is tied into your desire to connect with others. Sharing personal information is the best way to do that. But again, you may be sharing the wrong things."

Doug considered this.

"So," Penny said, "that's what I mean by a strength becoming a negative. No, I don't believe anyone is saying you have a flawed character. But your natural, good tendency and desire to talk and connect with people is just being expressed in the wrong way."

Doug thought a few moments and then said, "I get what you're saying, but c'mon, everyone gossips. Office gossip just goes with the workplace territory. It's social currency. Everyone does it."

"Maybe they do," Penny replied, "But, for better or worse, your role holds you to a higher level of accountability."

Doug didn't reply.

"Your job gives you access to all kinds of personal information," Penny said, "whether it's shared with you verbally or in a file or an employee review. And, because you have that kind of access, your words and behavior at the office have to be above reproach. And maybe that's not fair, but fairness isn't the issue."

Doug again didn't reply.

"Look, Doug," Penny said gently. "I'm not trying to browbeat you on this. You know me. I have no interest in hurting you or anyone else professionally. But we're here to discuss our feedback, so we might as well be honest, right?" Doug nodded slightly. "I tell you all of this because I'm concerned that, yes, your reputation may be suffering at the office. Okay?"

Doug again nodded.

"This issue is not about character," Penny said. "And, yeah, it may not be fair that you can't talk with people at the office like everyone else does. But the truth remains: When it comes to office gossip, you may have to settle for eagle status instead of hanging with the turkeys. "

Doug cracked a smile. "Nice imagery there."

Penny smiled back. "But it's true, Doug. You're better than that. You love talking to people, you love listening to people. But at times, you just get it all a bit twisted."

"Okay," Doug said, "So maybe it's not about character. But we're still talking about my reputation here. I'm known as the office gossip, and I can't exactly turn back time. I've got to live with that."

"That's true," Penny said. "That won't change overnight. It's going to take some time. And, it's a cliché, but trust just takes time."

"Right."

"But what's important is that you realize that your feedback isn't about bad character traits. It's about how your good character traits made a left turn."

Doug smiled.

"And," Penny continued, "the great thing about this issue is that it's an easy fix."

"Easy?" Doug laughed. "You mean all I have to do is change how I interact with other people? No problem," he said, snapping his fingers. "Done."

"Okay, not so easy," Penny said. "Maybe I should say, it potentially requires less work than some of the others. It's not initially about change, but self-restraint. Other behaviors—working behaviors—are tougher to address."

Doug glanced at her. "Are you speaking specifically or in general?"

Penny hesitated and replied, "Both."

Doug nodded. "Look, Penny, I know this sounds ridiculous after our conversation, but you really can talk to me about your report. I value our working relationship, and I would never talk about you to someone else. Really."

Penny nodded and said, "I know Doug, and I appreciate that."

"Look at it this way," Doug suggested. "You were able to help me with an issue that you don't personally struggle with. You're actually the most trustworthy person I know." He thought a moment and said, "Wait, are we together by design? Is Paige getting tricky on us?"

Penny laughed.

"Let's say she is," Doug said, smiling. "And let's assume that I may be able to help you the way you helped me. Maybe?"

Penny considered this, smiled and said, "Okay. Enough about you. Let's talk about me."

Chapter 15

Penny Wants to Improve

PENNY retrieved the 360 report from her computer bag.

"Doug, let me ask you a question."

"Okay."

"Did your feedback surprise you? Honestly."

Doug folded his hands and leaned back in his chair, clearly more comfortable than when they had started.

"Honestly? Yeah. Yeah, it did." He paused and said, "But really, does anyone ever view themselves in a critical light?"

"What do you mean?" Penny asked.

"Maybe it's just me, but don't we usually think it's everyone else that has the problem? I think we all find ways to justify our bad habits, our less-than-stellar choices. Our motives, and our behavior, aren't wrong. They're just misunderstood. Right?"

Penny smiled. "I would say that's true."

"So what about you?" Doug asked. "Was your report as shocking to you as mine was to me?"

Penny paused and said, "Actually, it wasn't shocking at all."

"Really?"

"Yes."

"The good and the, well, not so good?"

"Pretty much."

Doug grunted. "Well, you're more self-aware than me." He paused. "Than I."

"Maybe that's true," Penny said. "But self-awareness without action is pretty worthless."

"Okay," Doug said, slightly uncomfortable with Penny's immediate candor. He was also uncomfortable because a few of Penny's team members had, in both casual and official conversations, confided in Doug concerns about their boss. Whatever Penny's report contained, it probably would not surprise him either. "Why don't we talk about the strengths first."

"Okay." Penny flipped open the report binder. She found the first section and said, "Knowledge, flying colors. Leadership, high marks." She looked up and said, "Although, really, if I'm falling short in any of these areas, wouldn't that reflect poorly on me being a leader in general?"

Doug thought a moment. "Well, in the 360, Leadership focuses on specific characteristics. I mean, this whole thing is about leadership. But you can be good at leadership overall and still be imperfect in some areas."

"Imperfect? Me?" Penny laughed. "When I was in middle school and secondary school—or high school in the states—I received straight As. It was a foregone conclusion in my house that all of us kids would do well across the board."

"That sounds like fun."

Penny chuckled. "But that expectation made me perform. And you discover that you really can achieve whatever you actively pursue. I wasn't allowed to be either a Math or an English person. I had to be both." She held up the report. "So you can imagine how traumatizing it is to an overachiever to receive anything less than an A on a report card. Which is what the 360 feels like."

"It essentially is."

"Yes," Penny agreed. "But, even though I did well in school, I was a bit of a procrastinator. And once I got to college, with all of the distractions there, I began to procrastinate in earnest. I can't tell you how many times I stayed awake all night, finishing homework, or writing a report."

"Everyone pulls all-nighters in college," Doug pointed out.

"Yes, but I was *always* doing work at the last minute. I began to thrive on this artificial pressure that I had created for myself. I rationalized that I always did my best work when I was under the gun. Or maybe it just seemed that way because I had never done it any other way."

Doug nodded. He understood where this was going.

"And I carried that all-nighter attitude with me into the professional world." She glanced at the binder. "And here we are."

Doug said lightly, "So you received high marks on the 360 for procrastination?"

"In a way," Penny said. "Here's the rub. Yes, I do a good job. I get everything done on time. My team gets everything done on time. And the work and reports are almost always error free. But apparently my personal approach to timelines is really wearing thin in my group." She looked at Doug. "You remember Lateshia and Kenneth, of course."

"Sure." In particular, Doug remembered their exit interviews. Both had been worn out by Penny's last-minute approach to project timelines.

"Well, I would submit them as Exhibits A and B that my work style is challenging to the team. Lateshia was fantastic and able to handle everything I threw at her. And Kenneth had one of the sharpest minds I've encountered."

Penny gazed out the window and continued, "But I believe that they couldn't function anymore in the work environment I had created because it took their lives so out of balance. They had both joked with me about receiving too much work at the last minute. Or that I changed priorities too quickly. And I of course heard more detailed insights via other team members. So the fact is I inadvertently drove away some very talented people from Collier."

"Penny, I don't know if I would go that far. Both of them found opportunities elsewhere."

"Yes, they found new jobs. But they loved working at Collier. They completely caught Larry's vision for what we're about." She glanced at Doug and said, "Certainly you know all of this, Doug, since you conducted their exit interviews."

Doug shifted in his chair. "Yeah, but I, uh, can't really discuss that."

Penny smiled and nodded. "I know. But you do understand what I'm saying, though."

Doug shrugged and said, "Sure."

"So here's the bottom line: What works for me doesn't work that well for everyone else around me."

"But does it really work for you, too?" Doug asked.

"Sure. My job is about deadlines, and I have yet to miss one. No matter the stress, no matter the hours necessary, my reports will be on Larry's desk when he arrives that morning."

"I know, Penny. No one is concerned with the quality of your work or the timeliness of the delivery. But is that the most effective way to get it all done?"

"No, and I get that," she said, holding up the report. "I understand that I need to develop better systems for allocating and scheduling work among my team. This has made it very clear. It's unreasonable to expect my team to fit into my unorthodox way of working."

"But I think it's more than that, Penny," Doug pressed.

"And what is it?"

"This isn't just about making a better system for your team," Doug said. "That's a great and—by your own admission—much-needed change that will enhance their output, work environment, and morale."

"So what am I missing here?"

Doug paused and said, "You, Penny. You have to change."

"But this isn't about me, Doug," Penny said, slightly annoyed. "This is about working styles. Some people thrive under pressure, some need little guidance, and others need a more rigid structure. I just happen to have a very specific way of doing things. Of getting things done. And they do get done, every time."

"No one is questioning your results, Penny. They're questioning how you arrive at those results. This kind of change can't just be implemented with flow charts and schedules. Those are important. But these changes have to trickle down from the top. From you."

"Me? Completely change how I work? After all this time?"

Doug nodded. "I'm afraid so."

"Look, I've been doing things this way for years. Forever. This report is not going to magically change how I work. My primary responsibility to my team is to effectively lead them. And part of that is finding ways to create the best possible work environment for each of them. That's what the report is about.

"I rated well in every section aside from Execution," she continued. "That tells me that I'm by and large doing a good job. Yes, my way of executing tasks is negatively affecting them. So I need to create systems that allow each person to work in ways where they are most effective."

"I understand what you're saying, Penny," Doug said slowly. "I really do. But I have two points here."

"Okay."

"First, creating all of those systems for them is well and good, and is probably long overdue. But you are going to exist somewhere in that flowchart. You're still going to affect them no matter what, because you will always factor into their workflow. And if you're not functioning within those same parameters, those same standards that apply to everyone around you, it's just not going to work."

Penny didn't reply.

"Second," Doug rushed out. "If you're really honest with yourself, you can't truly believe that your way of doing things is the best way for *you*, too."

Penny again didn't reply.

"Yeah, your procrastination is affecting your team," Doug continued. "But it's also affecting you. I know you get the job done. You're amazing. A machine. You compress more work into a 48-hour marathon than I do in a full week. But since we're being honest here," he said, spreading his arms, indicating the room, "do you really think that's the best way to accomplish your goals and meet your deadlines?"

"Probably not," Penny conceded. "But it's just the way I'm wired."

"Maybe," Doug said. "Or maybe it's just the way you *learned* to do things."

"Okay, yes, it's how I've always done it," Penny said. "But think of what you're saying. What you're suggesting. That I completely change how I approach my job and workload. Can you imagine making such sweeping changes in your own life?"

"No." Doug laughed. "I didn't say it would be easy. I'm just saying it's probably necessary."

"It's like any habit," Penny said. "It's ingrained. It's even addictive. I *enjoy* the rush of working under a shotgun deadline."

"I know," Doug nodded. "But here's the thing. This 360 thing isn't really about finding indirect ways to make life better for our employees. Or how to improve their performance. It's not about improving departments. It's about improving *us*.

"Yes," Doug continued, "you could change the way in which you dole out responsibilities and how you create timelines for your team. But the real change that's needed isn't about any of that. It's about you making personal changes. Changes that will flow from you and *then* impact your team.

"Honestly?" Doug said. "Your team isn't suffering under an unorthodox work style. They're suffering from an *unrealistic* work style. From unrealistic expectations. And the only way you can change those expectations is by changing how you personally handle workloads."

Penny exhaled deeply. "I can't even fathom how I could change at this point."

"I get that. Believe me." Doug smiled. "As you said, I'm fortunate that I just have to keep my mouth shut."

Penny laughed. "Yeah, I want that change, please."

"But really," Doug said. "Every change in the report is difficult. Innovation? Building Talent? Professionalism? If anyone scored low in those categories, it's not because they're deliberately trying to perform poorly. Just like you, and just like me, they're going to have to fight a tough personal battle to make those changes. If all of this was easy, we wouldn't even need feedback or reports. And we wouldn't be working for a top notch company at an executive level."

"True." Penny thought a moment. "Like I said, I already knew what would be in my report before I even cracked it open. But seeing those thoughts on paper definitely changes things. And honestly, it's given me an urgency to address issues that I always felt were just fine staying under the rug. Success breeds complacency, right?"

"So they say."

Penny leaned back and watched the revelers outside. She smiled and joked, "I hope everyone is having as much fun as we are."

Chapter 16

Melissa is Stumped

MELISSA entered the small room and glanced around. A sofa faced the fireplace, while two wingback chairs were situated near a wall lined with a small collection of books. She walked to the chairs and took a seat.

Jim walked into the room and also looked around. "Cozy," he said. "Charming. Rustic. Not exactly what I had in mind for a meeting place."

Melissa placed her bag on the floor. "Maybe comfort inspires more honesty than sterility does."

"Maybe." He walked to the wall filled with books and perused the titles. The shelves featured a variety of subjects, from history, to sports, to the latest fiction. Jim slid a book out and turned it over, examining the back cover of a popular thriller.

"Have you read this?" he asked, holding up the book.

Melissa shook her head. "No. I read all the time, but not really for pleasure."

Jim placed the book back on the shelf. "You know, there are interesting things to discover and learn outside of technical manuals and trade magazines."

"Actually, correction. I read work-related things for pleasure." Melissa smiled sheepishly. "How sad is that?"

"Not sad," Jim said. "Just, er, committed."

Melissa laughed.

Jim sat down and set his bag on the floor. "So. Thoughts on the trip so far?"

Melissa considered the question and said, "It's been good. Interesting. My favorite part was taking an up-close look at our new panels, finally in operation. After all of the planning, design, and detail-work, it's rewarding to actually see the results."

Jim nodded. "And the resort's management team is thrilled with them. I got a chance to speak with the team this morning. They shared that they were pleased with the entire process, from consultation to installation. And your team played a big part in this, Melissa. You should be proud of what you, and they, have accomplished."

"I am. It's just kind of difficult to enjoy any of the success right now."

"Why is that?" Jim asked.

"Well," Melissa said and paused. "This 360 thing. It seems to be everywhere. It's even a part of this trip."

Jim nodded. "That's true. But what do you mean by everywhere?"

"For me, it's a part of most projects I'm working on. I'm constantly thinking, am I doing my job right? How do people perceive my work? Actually, that question was answered by my 360."

"Okay." Jim smiled. "So I guess we'll start with you."

Melissa sighed and took the 360 report out.

"First," Jim said, "I can't imagine that you received critical feedback across the board. You're too good at your job, too knowledgeable, and too hardworking for that to happen."

"This is true," Melissa agreed, smiling slightly. "It's actually just one glaring section."

"Well, then, what about the other six?"

"I did almost uniformly well," Melissa replied. She opened the report and scanned a few pages. "Fours and fives across the board." She glanced up and said shyly, "I almost had a perfect score in knowledge."

"Who could give you less than a five on that?" Jim asked, incredulous.

"I'm not sure." Melissa laughed. "Someone must have wanted to keep my head from swelling."

"Your knowledge *is* off the charts." Jim glanced at the books and said, "Your office could also serve as the unofficial library of alternative energy. And I'm betting you've read every book on the subject there."

"Some twice." Melissa laughed again.

"And that knowledge doesn't come easy," Jim pointed out. "Being an authority on something requires much more than reading books on the subject. I know you live and breathe both the grand design and minutiae of what we do. And that does not go unnoticed, unappreciated, or undervalued. You're such a significant part of the team, and you need to remember that. It can help you keep other issues in perspective."

"Thanks, Jim. I appreciate that. But my issues are viewed as being detrimental to the team. Not just the team, but the company. And to be honest, I don't even feel that my supposed issues are a problem. More like a misunderstanding. Or a positive viewed as a negative."

Jim nodded.

"That's what so tough about all of this," she continued. "I don't feel like people are singling me out. I don't feel like I'm being attacked. It's not that. I think everyone means well. But I don't believe they truly understand what I'm trying to do, and what I'm trying to avoid."

"Okay, so explain it to me."

Melissa flipped through her report. "So people seem to believe I'm lacking in Innovation. Or that I squash innovation, actually."

"Okay."

"People—my team, I'm assuming—believe that I'm too conservative and strict on projects. That I'm a control freak. That I micromanage and don't allow them room to work."

"Why do you think they feel that way?" Jim asked.

"I admit, I do understand how they could view me that way. But they need to understand that I'm responsible for every project that rolls out of our department. My approval causes projects to move forward. And because I'm accountable, it's vital that I am a part of every single detail of every single project. Doesn't that just make sense?"

Jim considered this and replied, "It does. To a degree. But you have a team for the very reason that you're supposed to distribute not only the workload, but the responsibility. The work and the responsibility need to go hand in hand."

"To a point, yes," Melissa agreed.

"Look at it another way," Jim said. "Larry is responsible for every department. Sales, engineering, production, all of it. But imagine if Larry was constantly trying to get involved in every single aspect of what we do. Imagine Larry visiting your office every hour and asking what you're working on. If he continually asked you to verify every detail, and confirm every finding. Would you enjoy that?"

"Definitely not."

"How would that affect your efficiency?" Jim persisted. "Your morale? Your progress?"

Melissa didn't reply.

"Wouldn't that make you feel like he believed you were incompetent? Like you couldn't be trusted?"

Melissa again didn't reply.

"It would also affect our time. Instead of doing your job, you'd continually be updating Larry on what you were doing." Jim paused and said, "And think of Larry. He would be exhausted trying to micromanage every one of his leaders. It would distract him from the greater responsibilities of his role.

"The same is true with you," Jim continued. "Micromanaging a team doesn't just affect productivity. It affects our immediate responsibilities and our overall leadership role. If we spend our time supervising every detail, we're not just a burden on our team, we're hurting our own ability to be effective.

"Larry has placed each of us in our roles because he trusts us to do the job," Jim said. "He doesn't want to worry about the details in sales, engineering, and everything else. That's why we're there. And that's why your team and project leaders are in their roles. To deal with the millions of details so you can focus on leading your team."

Melissa nodded slowly. "I get that, Jim. I do. But it's so much easier said than done. I trust my team, but I feel an overwhelming sense of responsibility. And that responsibility just comes out wrong, I guess."

"Right. Fortunately no one's asking for changes overnight. Right now, understanding the issue is the important first step."

Melissa sighed. "I have a few steps to make." She paused a moment and said, "Remember when we talked a few weeks ago? And I mentioned my meeting with Larry? About the WAV cell? I'm sure you've already heard about this."

Jim had indeed heard about the meeting, but he didn't reply.

"Larry asked me to make a last-minute change on the solar panels," Melissa said. "To change the cell components mere weeks before the panel was scheduled for production. I didn't want to do it. But Larry...well, he's Larry, so I did."

"And?" Jim asked, suppressing a smile, already knowing the answer.

Melissa rolled her eyes. "Yes, it was successful. No hiccups, no problems. But, what if there had been problems? It just so happens that we had a happy ending. But it could have gone another way."

"I can see that," Jim replied. "But Larry wasn't asking you to just take a reckless chance." He thought a moment and said, "You know, of course, that all great inventions and new ideas involve risk."

"Sure," Melissa replied. "But the end of a project is not the time for risks."

"But doesn't this situation refute that logic?" Jim challenged. "Look, opportunities are going to exist all along a project's timeline. Your perspective is that risk is only for the beginning. And why is that?"

Melissa mulled this.

"Because," Jim answered himself, "that's the way you've always done it."

Melissa didn't reply.

"But this issue isn't just about when to take a risk, Melissa. This issue is about your reluctance to *ever* take a risk. You know what works. You know what's proven. In fact, and in effect, you probably allow other companies to do the product testing for you. 'X and Y are proven effective, so they'll work for us.'"

Melissa again didn't reply.

"So here's the rub," Jim continued. "Larry wants to take risks that could allow Collier to lead. You prefer to stay within the worn path."

"Ouch."

"But am I right?" Jim asked.

"To a point," Melissa said. "But I don't agree with the semantics. I want to make safe choices that protect our products. That maintain our timelines. That deliver consistent products."

"And that's all admirable," Jim said. "However, Larry has a different vision. And, to be honest, a bigger vision. He doesn't just want to follow the path that others have created. He wants to blaze trails. And the only way that will happen is for Collier to take risks. Calculated risks, yes. But still risks."

Melissa considered this.

"This is a relatively new industry," Jim said. "The people at the front, like Collier, have the opportunity to be pioneers. It's like a group traveling through the woods without a map. Some people are afraid of that challenge. Others are invigorated by it. Some are going to lead, to take risks. Others are going to follow and stay comfortable. Larry knows where he wants to be. The question is, can you find a way to align your vision with his?"

Melissa sighed. "You're asking me if I can completely change my perspective."

"No," Jim said. "I'm not asking for change. I'm asking for acknowledgement. To acknowledge that it may be possible, and even beneficial, to take more risks in your job.

"The 360 is not about knee-jerk change," Jim observed. "It's about *recognition*, and *then* taking strategic steps to change. Change is what happens *after* the 360.

"So the question remains. Do you think you can find ways to catch Larry's vision for Collier? To understand his passion to not just create, but innovate? Because if you can latch onto his spirit and vision for Collier, change is going to follow."

Melissa was quiet a moment and then smiled. "Okay, Jim. You win. I can see your point. Points."

"I'm not trying to win," Jim said. "I just want to help."

Melissa nodded. "I know. And that's why I'm glad it's you in here." She paused and said, "You've really got this 360 thing figured out. How can I possibly help *you*?"

Jim chuckled. "I'm far from having anything figured out. It's easy to spot everyone else's issues. To be a genius with advice. It's our own issues that are tough."

Chapter 17

Jim Tries to Take His Feedback Well

JIM was unaccustomed to sharing his thoughts, much less his feelings, and certainly never his fears. Yet Melissa's candor was reassuring.

Still, he understood it might be awkward for Melissa to discuss relatively personal issues with a senior leader, especially since she had contributed to his 360 feedback. Perhaps more than anyone else at Collier, Melissa considered knowledge an essential component to effective leadership.

Melissa returned to the room, interrupting his thoughts, carrying two mugs of coffee. "Here you go," she said, handing him a cup.

"Thanks."

Melissa sat down in her chair and took a careful first sip. So far, the meeting had not been unpleasant. Yet Melissa was slightly apprehensive about Jim's part of the session. She had taken great efforts to honestly evaluate each leader, without bias, without prejudice. *Even Abby*, she thought with a small smile.

Melissa recognized that Jim was highly effective in almost every area of his role. Except for one. And it was no secret that Melissa highly valued knowledge.

Likewise, she understood that Jim—efficient, effective, deadline-driven—had been concerned about her micromanagement, risk aversion, and lack of flexibility. Yet Jim was a more senior-level leader and had greater reporting authority. Bottom line, it was unnerving to critique Jim, especially in a one-on-one setting.

Jim picked up on her anxiety and decided to break the ice.

"You know," he began, "I envy you, Melissa."

"Me?" Melissa said, startled. "How could you possibly be jealous of me? Do you remember what we just talked about? Apparently, I'm a mess."

Jim chuckled. "You're not a mess. You're like everyone else here. Practically perfect, just need a little work."

Melissa laughed. "Yeah, right."

Jim smiled. "This whole experience just highlights human nature. You can possess six areas of excellence and accolades, and all of those can be overshadowed in your mind by one area of critical feedback. It's amazing how anything critical can cause us to toss rational perspective out the window."

"Well, I admire that you've kept perspective on this."

"Oh, no," Jim said. "I'm a mess, too."

Melissa laughed.

"Rationally, I understand that keeping perspective is an important part of this process. But what human is truly and completely rational?"

"No one I know," Melissa responded. She paused then said, "So, why do you envy me?"

"I envy your staggering amount of knowledge about our products and our industry. And I'm jealous because, for you, learning doesn't seem to be a chore, but a pleasure. You have a natural impulse to get better by learning more."

"That's true." She smiled and said, "I don't read books so much as I devour them. There's just so much to learn."

"Exactly. That's exactly it." Jim thought a moment and said, "But what you see as a challenge, I see as something closer to impossible."

Melissa looked puzzled. "How so?"

"Well, maybe impossible is the wrong word. Perhaps ill-timed is more appropriate."

"Okay," Melissa said, waiting.

Jim thought a moment and then shifted gears. "You know, I'm not the sharing type. Sharing thoughts, sharing feelings, whatever." He smiled and said, "When you're in the military, or maybe it was just back then, you learn to keep your issues to yourself. Don't complain. Don't mope. Everyone's got their share of problems, and mine aren't much different than the next guy."

Jim gazed at the rows of books. "I'm an old-school kind of guy, Melissa. I'm sure that's no surprise. My time in the military really shaped who I am. It taught me some important lessons. It continues to inform my approach to a lot of things, from the personal to the professional. And overall, I would say that it's served me well. Get in, get the job done, no excuses.

"It's that training and experience that has made me good at what I do. Manufacturing draws on those strengths. Things must get done, period. There are extremely narrow, if any, margins for error. Little, if any, wiggle room for delays. You just have to do the job, without excuses.

"But now I'm starting to feel like a relic. An old-school guy in a very new-school world. I've always maintained that hard work and dedication are enough to achieve success. And, to an extent, they still are."

Melissa didn't reply, uncertain where this was going.

"But, more than anything else these past few weeks, I've learned that hard work isn't enough anymore. It's still 50% of any job. But there's another 50% that seems just as crucial. The ability to adapt. To learn new technologies. To even anticipate what's next. I've just got to figure that out without mounds of books to read."

Jim sipped his coffee. "Manufacturing has always been a great avenue for my strengths and my type of work ethic. But the world is changing, and the business world is *really* changing. Competitive doesn't even begin to describe it. If you react, you're already too late. We have to anticipate and be proactive.

"Deep down I understood this," Jim continued. "But I figured, 'Hey, I'm 58 years old, and I'm close enough to retirement that those changes won't affect me.' But these changes are moving faster than my aging."

"You should sell that," Melissa joked. "'Work in the high tech industry, slow down your aging process.'"

Jim laughed.

"See, we techies already know this secret," Melissa shared. "It's the reverse of dog years. For every human year, technology moves forward seven years. It's like the fountain of youth."

Jim laughed again. "Great. So I'm not a relic, I'm just aging slower. Perfect."

Melissa smiled.

Jim thought a moment. "Okay. Back to my original thought." He leaned back in his chair. "I'm sure you already know that Knowledge was my weakest area on the 360. I realized that before I even got my report back."

Melissa just nodded slightly, indicating she was listening, but not quite confirming his assumption.

"At first," Jim continued, "I thought, wait, I do my job. And manufacturing between industries is usually apples to apples, right? The details may differ, but the fundamentals remain the same.

"But I started to realize that, especially in this industry, knowledge is king. It's such a new field for everyone that we all need to be on top of what's happening. Everything is changing. The materials are evolving. The products are developing faster than ever before. Even the laws on renewable energy are changing."

Jim shook his head. "Sorry, I keep taking left turns." He laughed. "I'm saying all of this because, while I know that change is needed, I just don't know if I'll be able to adapt considering where I'm at in my career." He laughed again. "Whew, I finally got there."

Melissa smiled. "Well, Jim, I must respectfully disagree. I don't think you're a relic at all." She paused and said, "We're being honest here, right?"

He spread his arms. "By all means. Let me have it."

Melissa smiled again. "No, it's not like that. I don't think you believe you're incapable of learning, uh, new tricks." She laughed. "I think you're intimidated by the idea of *trying* to learn through books and technical manuals."

Jim nodded. "Yes, I think that's what I'm really trying to say. The idea of practically developing a new career for myself is daunting. I can't imagine learning as much as you. And reading all of those books? I would go crazy."

"That's just how I prefer to learn, though," Melissa pointed out. "You know, insular techie behavior."

Jim laughed.

"There are so many ways you could learn our business, Jim," Melissa continued. "You could start by reading industry magazines. Not too heavy, not too technical, but it would keep you informed on broader trends and issues."

"I'm listening."

"Conferences and seminars," Melissa suggested. "There are all kinds of these events taking place practically every week.

"But," she said, "you're overlooking the best resource you have."

"Which is?"

Melissa pointed to herself. "Us. I bet every single person on this retreat would be more than happy to share their knowledge with you. Who doesn't love to talk about what they know?"

"That's true."

"For example, I would love for you take part in some my team's meetings. Planning, R&D, testing. You name the meeting, I would welcome your presence. You don't even have to say anything. Or read anything. Just sit there and, you know, absorb our collective brilliance."

Jim laughed. "Who could refuse that offer?"

"There are so many ways you could learn about the industry in general and Collier in specific. Everyone I know thinks you're smart, committed, and hard-working. Those are great, super-important traits. But I think—no, I *know*—that you could enhance your role and presence at Collier by taking an active interest in the hows and whys of our products. It can only benefit you." She smiled and said, "I'm obviously the Knowledge cheerleader."

"You really are," he commented. "But you're right. It's not impossible. Just...overwhelming."

"But only at first, Jim," Melissa said. "Once you begin to understand the basic concepts of each product, material, and project, everything will naturally build from there. Play in the kiddy pool and you'll be swimming in the deep end in no time. I promise."

Jim chuckled. "Right."

Melissa pulled one leg under her and regarded Jim. "I've gotta say, you've certainly arrived at your personal epiphany much faster than I. I mean, it seems like you had a handle on this before you even walked into the room."

"I wouldn't call it quite an epiphany. But I've definitely been trying to look at the situation with an open mind." Jim thought a moment. He knew he could trust Melissa, but in sharing his discussion with

Larry, even hypothetically, he would be very close to moving from facts to conjecture. He carefully chose his words.

"Honestly, this has weighed on my mind in a few ways."

He paused then said, "When Larry first brought me to Collier, I was content to continue in what I knew best and coast into retirement. To finally trade ambition for consistency, and just enjoy my success. I still feel that way, actually."

Melissa nodded.

"But now I'm wondering if operations is really my final career stop. I've been wondering if I shouldn't prepare for what's possibly next."

Melissa's brow creased. Only one role at Collier could be Jim's next progressive step. She asked, "Wait, is Larry leaving the company?"

"No, no," Jim said quickly, casually, dismissively waving a hand. "Not at all. He loves Collier and plans to be here for the long haul."

Melissa settled back into her chair.

"Still, I need to be prepared for any potential growth, whatever that may be. I just want to be smart and plan accordingly."

Melissa nodded. "Well, it sounds like you've come to terms with your feedback. That's so great, Jim."

"Thanks," he said. "But I haven't arrived yet by any means. Understanding is one thing. Action is an entirely different challenge."

"Well, you certainly seem up to that challenge."

Just then Jim's phone buzzed. He leaned over his chair and stuck his hand in the bag, absently reaching for the phone. "Right. At least I hope so."

Chapter 18

Collier in Crisis

JIM sat alone in an armchair in his suite's bedroom, waiting for the phone to ring. Although it was still early Friday evening, he was already exhausted. The room was dim, illuminated by only the fading light outside and the glowing red numbers on a bedside clock radio. Jim didn't have the energy to do anything but sit in the dark and wait for the call. An earlier phone call had already changed everything.

After Larry's meeting with Paige, he had returned to his room to rest before the group reconvened. During that small window of time Larry had suffered a heart attack. Moments later Tina discovered him lying, though still conscious, on the bathroom floor. She immediately grabbed her purse, gave him 4 baby aspirin, and called 911. Everything between then and now seemed a blur.

Because the lodge was on a mountain and some distance from a major road, a medic helicopter was dispatched to the resort to take Larry to a hospital. Jim recalled standing on the helipad, the vehicle's rotating blades scattering the fresh snow, watching as the crew swiftly loaded Larry into the helicopter. Jim had offered to ride with them, but the medics insisted that only one person could travel with Larry, in this case, his wife. Jim watched as the helicopter lifted off the ground, and stood there long after the blinking lights sank beneath the tree line.

The leaders were initially in a state of panic. Everyone had met in the conference room, sitting in shocked disbelief. Shock gave way to concern, concern to planning, as they discussed the best course of action. They weren't scheduled to leave the resort until Sunday, which now seemed an eternity away. And while going home wouldn't help their situation, it would give each of them some sense of normalcy and the chance to take comfort in family and friends. So everyone was heading home the next morning. Twelve hours still seemed a relative eternity.

And so Jim waited for a phone call he was both anticipating and dreading.

■   ■   ■

TWO floors above Jim, the leadership team was sitting in the lodge restaurant, occupying a large round table near a fireplace. The dining room was situated on the resort's top floor, with large bay windows lining each wall, offering a stunning panoramic view of the surrounding hills. But the group was currently indifferent to their beautiful surroundings. The food was also ignored, as no one seemed to have an appetite.

Abby gave up on her salad and pushed away her plate. "I can't believe this is happening."

No one responded.

"Larry seems so healthy," Abby said. "Or I guess he just seems larger than life, you know? Impervious to something like this."

"Do we have any updates on his condition?" Doug asked.

Abby shook her head. "Not yet. Jim is waiting to get an update from Tina. The medics said it appeared he had a heart attack."

No one responded. Everyone was too anxious to really talk about anything, and worried about events they couldn't control.

⬛　⬛　⬛

PAIGE sat in the living room of her suite, cradling a mug of coffee as she watched the snow fall outside her window. Her room faced the slopes, normally a scene of flurried activity, now still and quiet at this hour. A brilliant moon shone down and lit up the white landscape.

The team had invited her to dinner, but Paige had politely declined. While she was familiar with each leader, and they in turn seemed comfortable with her, Paige felt they needed time to privately discuss what they were experiencing as a group. She didn't want to upset that dynamic. The events that day were more personal than professional, and Paige thought it best to bow out of those conversations. Her specialty was leadership development, not crisis management.

Yet Paige understood that the two subjects were intertwined. It was in times of crisis that solid, confident leadership was critical to keeping a team on track. Certainly, the most pressing concern was Larry's health. But the time was quickly coming when the group would need to address issues and concerns that would result from the crisis.

Paige sipped her coffee. Leaders didn't have the luxury of wallowing in anxiety and worry, or allowing others to make tough decisions for them. Back at Collier, hundreds of people would be directly impacted by their choices. The entire company would look to them for confident, courageous leadership in the weeks and months ahead.

As part of her leadership development curriculum, Paige often placed team members in a hypothetical crisis, like an Earthquake or a downed airplane. The group was given a critical event, a set of circumstances, and options for addressing their situation. It encouraged teams to collectively make decisions, to work together, and to discover personal strengths and weaknesses.

Collier's team was now facing a very real crisis. She hoped for Larry's swift recovery. She hoped for his eventual return to Collier. And she hoped his team would rise above this tragedy and press on. Time would tell.

■   ■   ■

JIM'S phone buzzed and he snatched it up. "This is Jim."

He heard a weary voice. "Jim, it's Tina."

"Tina! What's going on? How is Larry?"

"He's doing okay," Tina said. "He's currently sleeping. They think the baby aspirin helped save his life. The doctors have examined him, and they say the heart attack appears to have caused only minor damage."

Jim leaned back in his chair. "I'm so glad to hear that. Everyone has been really worried."

"I hear you. So, yeah, he's doing well. As well as could be expected, I'm told. So that's a relief."

Jim nodded to himself.

"Anyway," Tina continued, "that's really all I know for now. Larry will be staying here for a few days so they can run some more tests. But the prognosis is favorable."

"That's great, Tina. Just great. How are you holding up?"

"I'm trying. The kids flew in, and they're here with me, so that helps. Right now I'm just going to try to get some rest. I feel like I haven't slept in two days."

"You probably haven't," Jim replied. "So I'll let you go. But thank you for calling me with the update. I know everyone will be relieved."

"Yes," Tina said. "I mean, he's not completely out of the woods yet, but the doctors are fairly optimistic."

"Okay, get some sleep. And please call me with any updates."

"I will, Jim. Talk to you later."

Jim looked through the window. He needed to call the rest of the team with the news. Yet he paused a moment, taking in the falling snow.

While Jim was relieved to learn that his friend and his boss was going to be okay, he knew that things would be changing at the office. He had no doubt that Larry would return when he was healthy. Retirement wasn't in Larry's vocabulary. Yet he wouldn't be back immediately, which meant there would have to be some short-term adjustments to the leadership team.

Jim recalled his meeting with Larry a few weeks ago, where they had discussed the possibility of Jim eventually leading the company. He hadn't given it much thought since then. But now he realized that what he had first considered a long-term opportunity could become an immediate reality.

Chapter 19

Rising to the Occasion

GREG ANDERS stood and greeted Jim Sroka.

"Jim," Greg said. "Good morning."

"Good morning," Jim replied, shaking Greg's outstretched hand.

"Have a seat," Greg said, indicating a chair facing his desk.

Greg's assistant entered and placed a serving tray on Greg's desk. The tray held a carafe and two porcelain coffee mugs.

"Coffee?" Greg asked, pouring himself a cup.

"Thanks," Jim replied. He felt anxious about this meeting. Still the agenda was straightforward: Determine the interim leadership plan during Larry's leave of absence. Actually Greg already had the plan in mind. Jim was here to learn just what that plan entailed.

Greg propped his elbows on the desk and cradled his coffee. "As you know," he began, "Larry's prognosis is positive. The doctors expect a complete recovery relatively quickly."

Jim nodded. "Yes. Great news."

"Wonderful news. However, they've recommended that he take 90 days after his procedure to fully rest and recuperate. Larry," Greg smiled, "grudgingly agrees with this assessment. He would come back tomorrow if it were up to him. But he also knows this is the best way to ensure a full recovery."

Jim again nodded. "Right."

"So," Greg said, "now that we've dealt with the most pressing issue, which is getting Larry back to health, the next issue is the leadership plan for this period." Greg set down his mug and said, "Jim, I want you to serve as interim president during this time."

Jim discreetly exhaled. He had privately expected this decision. But now here it was, in the open and very real.

"Greg, I'm flattered," Jim replied. "And I'm happy to serve in any way necessary."

Greg nodded. "I knew I could count on you, Jim." He glanced at the reports and files on his desk and said, "We have a lot of ground to cover. Think you can spare a few hours with me today to get things up and running?"

"Of course." But his confident response hid his apprehension. Jim's moment of truth had arrived. He felt prepared, but would also need the full cooperation of the team to be effective. Jim wondered what that cooperation would look like.

■   ■   ■

JIM stepped into his office and closed the door. He had just finished a four-hour marathon meeting, during which Greg had covered Collier's most immediate concerns including appropriate communication to investors and other stakeholders. Jim had left Greg's office feeling overwhelmed.

He slid into his office chair and leaned back. Jim couldn't escape the similarities between this situation and his leadership conversation with Larry. It had only been a few days ago, but with everything that had happened, it felt more like months.

He remembered Larry's talk of succession, which Jim hadn't taken very seriously at the time. Like any big change, Jim mentally placed it far down the timeline. Two years, maybe, allowing him to naturally grow into the role. But he never could have imagined that things would change this quickly. And while it wasn't a permanent promotion, it still placed Jim in a position for which he didn't feel entirely qualified.

Knowledge. In the course of a few days, Jim's small problem had grown into a full-blown issue. When it came to company knowledge, Jim had believed he had time on his side. Now, incredibly, that time was up.

Knowing then what he knew now, Jim would have aggressively pursued learning from day one. But he realized that it wouldn't do any good to dwell on his initial resistance toward gaining industry knowledge. The time for thinking had passed. Action was now his only course.

Jim got up and left his office.

And here we go.

　　　　■　　■　　■

JIM knocked on Abby's open door.

Abby looked up from her monitor. "Jim. Hi. Come on in."

"Hi, Abby," Jim said, taking a seat across from her.

"You doing alright?" Abby asked.

"I am, thank you. You?"

"Business as usual." She smiled and added, "Or, the usual business in unusual times."

"I hear you," Jim said. "You've heard about Larry's favorable prognosis, of course."

"I have, yes. Such a relief."

Jim nodded. "Listen, Abby, Greg isn't announcing this until tomorrow, but I wanted to talk with you today. To keep things moving forward with minimal speed bumps."

Abby furrowed her brow and said, "Okay."

"As you know, Larry is taking 90 days to recuperate. And during this time, Greg has appointed me to serve as the interim president."

Abby slowly nodded. "Congratulations, Jim."

"Thanks, Abby."

Abby remarked, "It says a lot about you that Greg wants you in that role."

"It does," Jim agreed. "But, honestly, I have a lot of work in front of me to get up to speed. Regardless, I'm ready to do whatever's necessary to best serve Collier and the team."

"I know you are. That's great, Jim."

"And," Jim continued, "that's why I'm here. I may technically be in charge, but I can't do this without the entire team. The only way I can make this work is if I'm able to draw from each person's talents and knowledge."

Abby nodded.

Jim continued, "This is probably long overdue, but, if you wouldn't mind, I would like to sit in on some of your team meetings."

"Of course, Jim. Not a problem. We'd love to have you there."

"I won't be there to oversee what you're doing. I'll be there to learn."

Abby looked surprised. "Oh?"

Jim nodded. "It's a step I should have taken months ago. Probably back when I first started. You and your team have an incredible range of knowledge about our products and buyers, and I would love to just sit there and soak it all up."

Abby's processed this and said, "Absolutely, Jim. I can show you our upcoming schedule, or you can just contact Brooke when it's convenient."

"I'll probably check with Brooke tomorrow," Jim said, standing. "Right now I've got to continue my mini tour."

"Oh yeah?" Abby replied. "Well, you're off to a positive start."

*   *   *

JIM knocked on Melissa's office doorframe.

Melissa looked up from a report and smiled. "Hi, Jim. How are you?"

"I'm well," Jim said, taking a seat. "You?"

"Super busy," Melissa replied. "Have you heard more about Larry?"

"Yes," Jim replied. "He's doing well and the doctors are very positive about his progress. But to make sure he fully recovers, they advised that Larry take a 90-day leave of absence."

Melissa nodded. "That's good news."

"It is."

"So." Melissa paused and asked, "What's the plan in the meantime?"

"Well, that's one reason I'm here. I met with Greg today and he asked me to serve as the interim president during Larry's recovery. He's announcing it tomorrow."

Melissa smiled. "Good for you, Jim. I know you'll do an incredible job."

"Thank you," Jim said. "But this won't be a one-man show. I have so much ground to cover, and I'll only be able to do it with the help of every leader here."

"Of course," Melissa replied. "I'm glad to help in any way I can."

"Which leads me to the second reason I'm here," Jim said. "I need to immerse myself in every aspect of Collier's business. To learn as much as I can in a very short period of time. And, since I'm not a product expert such as yourself, I will rely heavily on your recommendations." He added, "And support."

Melissa look surprised. "Wow. Thanks, Jim. That's kind of you to say."

"Well, it's the truth." Jim leaned forward and said, "I've found every reason to avoid learning about our business. Or should I say, every excuse. But excuses won't cut it now." He smiled and referenced her remark from their dyad session at the retreat. "I have no choice but to skip the kiddy pool and jump right into the deep end of the knowledge pool."

Melissa smiled in understanding.

"Anyway," Jim said. "The excuses are over. So here I am. And I'd like to take you up on your offer to sit in on some meetings with your team."

"By all means," Melissa said. "You're welcome to attend any of our meetings."

Jim nodded. "And as a part of my education, if you're able to spare any time, I'd like to talk with you about industry trends, news, whatever. If you think it's relevant to Collier and what we're doing, I'd like to hear about it."

"Of course, Jim. Anytime."

Jim nodded and stood. "I'll be in touch with you soon to set up a meeting. Thanks for your help on this."

As Jim reached the door Melissa said, "Jim?"

He turned and said, "Yeah?"

"You're going to do great."

■　　■　　■

JIM knocked on Paige's open office door.

"Jim," Paige greeted him, putting down her pen. "So good to see you."

"Thanks," Jim replied. "How's it going?"

"Well," she said. "How about you?"

"Good," he said. "Got a minute?"

"Of course," Paige said, indicating a chair.

Jim settled in the chair. "Greg is announcing this tomorrow. During the interim while Larry is recovering, I'll be acting as Collier's president."

"Congratulations," Paige said. "I know you'll do a wonderful job."

"I hope so. There's a lot of work ahead. And I feel a bit overwhelmed."

"I know you'll rise to the occasion, Jim." Paige smiled and added, "I've seen your dossier."

Jim smiled in return. "Actually, I'm here because of that. Because I want to thank you."

"Really? What for?"

"The work you've been doing. Specifically, the work you've done with me."

"It's probably no surprise," Jim continued, "but I wasn't initially thrilled with my 360 Report or the recommendations to improve."

Paige nodded.

"But," Jim said, "the reality is the 360 made me take an honest look at who I am. It made me face an issue that, until then, until now, I had believed was a nonissue."

Jim paused and remarked, "It's unfortunate that it takes a crisis to deliver a wake-up call. And it's terrible that it took a colleague's serious health problem to force me to make changes. But I guess all of life is like that, right?"

"It does seem that way," Paige agreed. "And we're all like that."

Jim nodded. "While I'm not happy about how this came about, I'm glad I'm in the hot seat. The choice is gone, you know? I can't afford to avoid learning about the specifics of our business. So while it's been long overdue, I'm ready to begin."

"That's great, Jim. I'm happy to hear you say that."

Jim stood to leave and said, "I'm certainly not all the way there yet. But I've made the decision to learn as much as I can. I don't want the company to sit in neutral during Larry's absence. I hope to hand Collier back to Larry in even better shape than when he left. But there's a lot of hard work to be done to get there."

"Lucky for you, the entire team will help you get there."

Chapter 20

Dynamic Growth

LARRY WESLEY drove into Collier's parking garage and found his designated spot. Although it had been only a little over three months since he last entered the building, it seemed a lifetime ago.

Larry pulled the car into his space and, as always, noticed the sign bearing his name. He stared at the wall and felt a mixture of emotions. He was excited to be back, eager to get started, anticipating the day ahead. At the same time he felt anxious, even nervous. Larry broke his stare, got out of the car, and entered the building entrance.

The security guard looked up from his desk and said, "Welcome back, Mr. Wesley."

"Thanks." Larry paused in mid-step and said, "Thank you..." He cocked his head, searching for a name he didn't know, looking for a name tag, even encouraging the guard to fill the gap.

"Jason."

"Right. Thanks, Jason." Larry entered an open elevator and pressed his floor. As usual he examined himself in the mirrored doors. Everything looked the same, but everything was different.

◼   ◼   ◼

THE elevator doors parted, slowly revealing a room full of people, the small lobby overflowing with his coworkers. Team leaders, executives, administrative staff, even Greg. Everyone was there to welcome him back. As Larry walked off of the elevator, he was greeted by applause and cheers.

Larry stood in front of the elevator, experiencing a wave of emotions. He was truly touched by the public and enthusiastic support of his people. Greg broke away from the group and shook Larry's hand. Greg threw his other arm over Larry's shoulder and turned to face the group.

"Team," Greg said, "I would just like to welcome back our very own Larry Wesley."

The group wildly applauded while some whistled.

Greg waited for the noise to fade and said, "Needless to say, I am thrilled that Larry is back with us. He is indispensible to me, and to Collier. We've definitely felt his absence."

The group offered more applause.

Greg continued, "I also want to publicly recognize Jim Sroka for his outstanding leadership during this crucial period. Jim had very big shoes to fill, but he did a wonderful job of getting up to speed and keeping us moving forward." He extended a hand toward Jim and said, "So thank you, Jim." Everyone in the room applauded.

Greg turned to Larry and said, "Larry, would you like to say anything?"

"Yeah," Larry replied and then cracked, "Jim, do I get my office back?"

The group laughed, knowing that moving into Larry's office had never once crossed Jim's mind.

         ▨   ▨   ▨

PAIGE approached Natalie Long's desk, causing her to reflect on her initial visit to Larry's office. Paige wondered how this meeting would differ from their first.

"Good morning, Paige," Natalie replied. "You can go right in, he's expecting you."

"Thanks," Paige said and entered Larry's office. Larry was on the phone, and he held up his index finger to Paige, silently asking for a moment. Soon afterward, Larry hung up the phone and stood to greet Paige.

"Sorry, the phone has not stopped ringing." Larry said, extending his hand. "Good to see you."

"You, too," Paige replied, shaking his hand. She held his hand for another moment and said, "You look great. Ready to take on the world."

Larry smiled. "That's actually the first item on today's to-do list. Have a seat."

"I would believe it," Paige replied. She paused then said, "So."

"Yes. So," Larry said. "First thing, I want to thank you for your time with Collier."

"Of course. It was a pleasure."

Larry smirked. "Not always, I imagine."

"It was. You have a great team, Larry. I know you are proud of them."

Larry nodded. "I do, and I am." He continued, "I haven't been back long, of course. But I've already heard from all of my leaders. And each of them said they've been working on their development which all started with the 360." He added, "But I'm not going to have

another heart attack the next time we need a kick in the pants. Just
so you know."

Paige played along. "You *did* get everyone's attention. That was
above and beyond, Larry." She added seriously, "But everyone pulled
together, and the best of your team showed up. More importantly,
you have a team that is sustainable. They know their strengths, their
blind spots, and when they need to ask for help and feedback from
each other."

Larry nodded. "Big strides. I appreciate all you've done to help
our team. Listen, I'm having my first official meeting with the leadership team today and I'd like you to join us."

"I'd love to. What time?"

"2 p.m."

■   ■   ■

LARRY entered the conference room and, for the second time
that day, was greeted by applause. Larry smiled and waved his hands.
He glanced around the table and saw that every leader was already
there. They were glad to have him back, and it felt good. Paige sat in
her now customary chair at the end of the table.

After everyone had quieted down, Larry addressed the group
enthusiastically, "Good afternoon, everyone. It's already been a wild
day. I'm ready for my next leave-of-absence."

Everyone laughed.

"I've called you all here for a state-of-the-company address." He
paused. "Or, more accurately, a state-of-the-president."

"First, about my situation. My doctors have given me the go-ahead
to come back to work full time. Actually, I've recovered rather well,
but I'm going to have to change some of my wicked ways. Less sitting,
more exercise. Less body fat, healthier foods. Fewer 60-hour work
weeks, more down time." He added with a grin, "Generally, less fun.

"Old ways die hard. But I know I'm fortunate to be here, so I'm willing to do what's necessary to keep me healthy."

He surveyed the table. "Not every change will be limited to lifestyle, though. As you can imagine, an event like this makes a big impression. You don't exactly come back the same way you left.

"And," he continued, "three months of unemployment gives you a lot of time to think." He added, "Probably too much time."

He paused again. Everyone waited, each growing more curious as to where this meeting was going.

Larry said, "Not to get melodramatic—because I don't do soap opera well—but a close call can offer a new perspective on things. This event brought my life into focus. I've always heard this but that reality doesn't sink in until you experience it for yourself." He paused and smiled. "I promise I'm going somewhere with this.

"My point is this: My situation has given me some clarity. My priorities have been re-evaluated. Professionally, Collier is still my top priority. That hasn't changed. But while I still want Collier to be successful, *how* we get to that success seems just as important as actually reaching our goals.

"I want Collier to be the industry leader. And I want our leadership team to be the best in the industry. And why not? We can do it."

Larry indicated Paige and said, "After a lot of thought on this, I've realized that Paige brought us an effective catalyst for sparking personal growth. Like it or not, professional growth is intrinsically tied directly to personal growth. You can't separate the two worlds.

"This was my biggest issue with the 360. I didn't want to accept that truth. I wanted to believe that my personal issues had no influence on my professional life. But now, I get it. Or at least I'm starting to get it.

"Now, am I going to radically change overnight? Not a chance." Everyone chuckled. "No one does. But I recognize that we can't run from our weaknesses. We can't avoid ourselves. And I don't want to be responsible for sweeping issues under the boardroom rug.

"So," Larry said, "here is my pledge to all of you. I'm going to do my best to take an honest and consistent look at my areas of weak—," he glanced at Paige and corrected himself. "Opportunities." Everyone smiled.

"And I'm asking all of you to join with me in that attitude. Again, I'm not expecting for everyone to make radical, immediate changes. I'm asking for open minds. And I'm asking everyone here, myself included, to find ways to constructively and honestly encourage growth in your teams.

"To that end, I'm planning on having Paige make scheduled visits throughout the year to help us walk through that process. We are looking for progress, not perfection." He looked around. "So, does that sound feasible?" Everyone around the table nodded.

"Okay," Larry said, clapping his hands. "Stay tuned. But for now, let's get back to it. And I will be open to your feedback. In fact, I *invite* your feedback."

■   ■   ■

EVERYONE lingered after the meeting to personally welcome back Larry. Each leader filtered out until only Larry and Paige remained.

"Well, Larry," Paige said, "I have to say, I'm impressed."

"Right," Larry said. "But don't worry. I'm still Larry. That was as touchy feely as I get."

Paige laughed. "No doubt."

Larry and Paige left the conference room and walked toward his office. Larry glanced at Paige and said, "So, where to next?"

"Home," Paige replied. "I have two days of downtime."

"Two entire days?"

"I know," Paige said. "I bet you can relate."

"I can."

"But I love it here," Paige said. "Working with talented and ambitious people, helping them become more successful, does it get better than that?" She paused and asked, "So how's that for touchy feely?"

"Hey," Larry said. "After these last three months, touchy feely doesn't seem like a waste of time."

"You know Larry, I may actually agree with that sentiment."

Larry laughed. "Whoa. Aren't you still on the clock?"

※　※　※

LARRY entered his office and stood near the doorway. He was thrilled to be back and wanted to take in the room, the furniture, the view, everything.

Larry moved behind his desk and sat down. From the corner of his eye Larry noticed the 360 assessment wedged under other office reports. He pulled the report out and glanced at it. Larry opened the lower drawer of his desk to store the binder, but continued holding the report, wavering.

He shut the drawer and stood, walking over to a bookcase facing his desk. Larry slid the report in between other binders and began to walk away, but turned around. He walked back and found another space on the shelf, room for the report to rest with the cover facing forward, bold letters stating "360 Assessment: Larry Wesley, President." He nodded slightly and returned to his desk.

Larry wanted a reminder. A reminder that his team needed and deserved the best possible leadership. A daily reminder that change was a daily process. Even a reminder of some of the darkest moments of his life, both personal and professional. He was determined to become the kind of boss that he would want to work for.

But he had already experienced the worst days of his career. Now Larry was preparing for the best.

Next Steps

A Self-Administered 360-Degree Assessment©

The next 8 steps:

1. Please complete the assessment yourself first.

2. Then identify the right people who can provide you feedback. Choose people who know you, and who influence and impact you. As you put together your list of 6 to 10 peers, direct reports, colleagues, and your boss or supervisor, make sure they can provide you with honest and developmental feedback.

3. Don't populate your list with only outliers—either those who don't have your best interest at heart, or raving fans with rose-colored glasses. Include the middle of the bell curve, those who care about you and the company and have some insights into how you can become more successful. Then make your first face-to-face or phone appointment with each person. Our recommendation is to provide the 28 Questions ahead of your appointment so the raters can consider their responses.

4. View this 360 process as a series of conversations with people who care about you. It is not a test. There is no pass/fail or right/wrong. These questions are all conversation starters. So it takes courage and a willingness to listen. When you receive feedback, don't jump in, interrupt, and justify. Just listen carefully.

5. Set up each session for no more than 30 minutes. If it goes longer, fine. But this isn't a counseling session—it's a friendly, professional discussion on your strengths, your development areas, and your potential. Make sure you have water or coffee available. Hospitality makes everyone more comfortable.

6. When we provide **The Bixler 360-Degree Feedback Report**© in our coaching and consulting practice, there is both a numerical response and an essay portion. In this Self-Administered version, you will ask each member in your group to provide a response with a rating between 1 and 10. Otherwise, it is too vague and not very helpful. But also ask for explanation. That's the beauty of a feedback conversation—it is a dialogue, not a one-way conversation.

7. This process will give you a customized roadmap to professional insight and personal growth. Knowing how others see us is a tremendous gift. It allows you to craft a better life and a more rewarding career.

8. Continue to check The Power of Feedback website *(www.the poweroffeedback.com)* for more ideas on your development.

Bixler Self-Administered 360-Degree Assessment©:

Name: _____

Rater: _____

Thanks for taking the time to provide feedback to me. When we meet, please use a rating system of 1 to 10 for your feedback with 1 (low) and 10 (high). This will provide more clarity and help me better understand my strengths and areas of development.

Leadership:

_____ 1. Do I set clear and realistic expectations for what is required?

_____ 2. Do I deploy resources—people, money and time—appropriately?

_____ 3. Do I hold myself accountable and do what I commit to?

_____ 4. Do I help create an engaging and motivated workplace?

General Comments on my leadership:

Knowledge:

_____ 5. Do I stay current in the industry and the market place?

_____ 6. Do I access my team when I need new ideas?

_____ 7. Am I considered a subject matter expert by my customers and colleagues?

_____ 8. Do I seek and promote continuous learning?

General Comments on my knowledge of the business:

Innovation:

_____ 9. Do I actively look for new ideas and innovative approaches for the business?

_____ 10. Do I encourage creativity within my team?

_____ 11. Do I apply new information, skills, and methods that move the business forward?

_____ 12. Do I take enough risks?

General comments on my use of innovation:

Building Talent:

____ 13. Do I keep my team members engaged and challenged?

____ 14. Do I consistently mentor and encourage my team members?

____ 15. Do I "walk the talk" and provide role modeling?

____ 16. Do I provide cross-training and opportunities for professional growth for myself and others?

General comments on my effectiveness on mentoring and building talent:

Trustworthiness:

____ 17. Do I show good judgment and demonstrate honesty and openness?

____ 18. Do I avoid negative politicking and conflicts of interest?

____ 19. Do I show fairness in my dealings with others?

____ 20. Am I open to feedback and accepting responsibility for my own mistakes?

General comments on character:

Professionalism:

_____ 21. Do I create a credible and confident presence?

_____ 22. Do I communicate professionally in email, text, memos, and other written communication?

_____ 23. Do I communicate professionally in presentations, staff meetings, phone calls, and other verbal communication?

_____ 24. Do I listen well?

General comments on my professionalism:

Execution:

_____ 25. Am I effective at prioritizing my activities?

_____ 26. Do I spend the majority of my time in the areas that move the business forward?

_____ 27. Do I communicate what is most important to my team so they work on the right issues?

_____ 28. Do I get results?

General comments on my commitment and effectiveness to getting things done:

CPSIA information can be obtained at www.ICGtesting.com
Printed in the USA
LVOW030804201011

251200LV00003B/1/P